KIDS' COOKING FUN

Publications International, Ltd.

MESSAGE TO PARENTS

Children, like adults, feel positive about an experience if they are successful. JELL-O KIDS' COOKING FUN has been designed with children's cooking success in mind.

Each recipe has the ingredients and equipment highlighted in colored boxes to make it easy for the child to assemble everything he or she will need before beginning. The recipes are written in carefully illustrated steps so they are easy to follow. JELL-O MAN (the children's hero who saves their JELL-O gelatin and pudding from thieves) and his loyal dog WOBBLY help explain the steps of each recipe.

The first chapter of the book is called "The Real Easy Stuff," and it contains recipes for "Plain Gelatin" and "Plain Pudding." We encourage you to direct your child to those recipes first, as they are the building blocks for all the other recipes in the book. Once your child has mastered these, he or she can have fun making any of the other recipes.

Of course, you will want to make sure your child uses safe kitchen techniques. Spend time reading through and making sure your child understands "Rules of the Kitchen" on page 4. All recipes requiring adult supervision are clearly marked with appropriate symbols (see page 4 for explanation of these symbols) so that you will be able to clearly identify which recipes your child can make alone and which ones will require your help.

So tie on your aprons, review the "Rules of the Kitchen" with your child and have fun!

Copyright © 1991 Kraft General Foods, Inc.
All rights reserved.

ANGEL FLAKE, BAKER'S, COOL WHIP, JELL-O, JELL-O MAN, JIGGLERS, KRAFT and WOBBLY are trademarks of Kraft General Foods, Inc., Glenview, IL 60025.

UNO® is a registered trademark of International Games, Inc.

Pictured on front cover (*left to right*): Funny Face Desserts (*page 14*); Ice Cream Shop Pies - Pistachio Chocolate Bar Pie and Rocky Road Pie (*page 94*); Gelatin Pizza (*page 46*).

Pictured on back cover (*clockwise from top left*): JIGGLERS Birthday Dessert (*page 68*); Funny Face Desserts (*page 14*); Cookies & Cream Pudding Pie (*page 90*); Funny Face Desserts (*page 14*).

Library of Congress Catalog Card Number: 91-61024

ISBN: 0-88176-654-2

This edition published by Publications International, Ltd., 7373 North Cicero Avenue, Lincolnwood, IL 60646

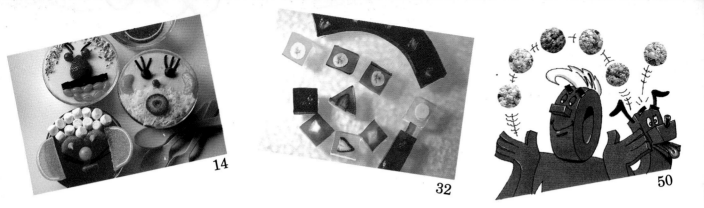

14

32

50

TABLE OF CONTENTS

56

68

84

4 **TAKE** pan out of refrigerator. Put about 1 inch of warm water in sink. Dip **just bottom** of pan into warm water for 15 seconds.

5 **USE** cookie cutters to cut gelatin into any shapes you wish. (If you do not have cookie cutters, cut gelatin into squares with a table knife.) Lift shapes out of pan with your fingers.

Makes about 24 small shapes

Use any leftover pieces to make "Scrap Happy" (see page 40).

JIGGLERS "SURPRISES"

<table>
<tr><td>

INGREDIENTS

4 packages (4-serving size each) OR 2 packages (8-serving size each) JELL-O Gelatin, any flavor

2½ cups boiling water

36 "surprises," such as: banana slices, strawberry halves, canned pineapple chunks

</td><td>

EQUIPMENT

Medium mixing bowl
Measuring cup
Rubber scraper or large spoon
13 x 9-inch pan
Table knife

</td></tr>
</table>

1 **POUR** gelatin into bowl. Add 2½ cups boiling water to gelatin. Stir with rubber scraper until gelatin is completely dissolved, about 2 minutes. Pour into 13 x 9-inch pan.

2 **LET** pan of gelatin stand on counter for 30 minutes. Gelatin will become thickened.

3 **ARRANGE** "surprises" in rows in thickened gelatin so that, when cut, each square will have a surprise. Put pan into refrigerator to chill until firm, about 3 hours. Take pan out of refrigerator.

4 **PUT** about 1 inch of warm water in sink. Dip **just bottom** of pan into warm water for 15 seconds. With table knife, cut gelatin into shapes, making sure you have a piece of fruit in each shape. Lift shapes out of pan with your fingers.

Makes about 36 small shapes

Use any leftover pieces to make "Scrap Happy" (see page 40).

JIGGLERS ALPHABET

INGREDIENTS	EQUIPMENT

INGREDIENTS

4 packages (4-serving size each) OR 2 packages (8-serving size each) JELL-O Gelatin, any flavor

2½ cups boiling water

EQUIPMENT

Medium mixing bowl
Measuring cup
Rubber scraper or large spoon
13 x 9-inch pan
Paper and pencil
Alphabet cutters
Tray or large plate

1 **POUR** gelatin into bowl. Add 2½ cups boiling water to gelatin. Stir with rubber scraper until gelatin is completely dissolved, about 2 minutes.

2 **POUR** into 13 x 9-inch pan. Put pan into refrigerator to chill until firm, about 3 hours. Take pan out of refrigerator. Put about 1 inch of warm water in sink. Dip **just bottom** of pan into warm water for 15 seconds.

3 **WRITE** down on a piece of paper the words you wish to use. Then, use alphabet cutters to cut out each JIGGLERS letter you need. Lift letters out of pan with your fingers. Arrange letters into your words on a tray.

Makes about 25 (2-inch) letters

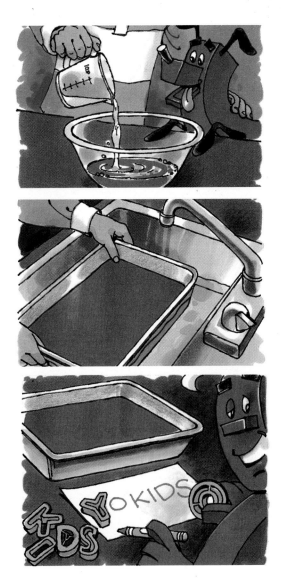

Use any leftover pieces to make "Scrap Happy" (see page 40).

Can you make a sentence from these words? (Answer is on page 40.)

JIGGLERS SAILBOAT

INGREDIENTS

4 packages (4-serving size each) OR 2 packages (8-serving size each) JELL-O Gelatin, Orange Flavor

2½ cups boiling water

4 packages (4-serving size each) OR 2 packages (8-serving size each) JELL-O Gelatin, Lime Flavor

2½ cups boiling water

COOL WHIP Whipped Topping, thawed, if you wish

EQUIPMENT

2 medium mixing bowls

Measuring cup

Rubber scraper or large spoon

2 (13 x 9-inch) pans

Table knife

Metal or plastic spatula

Paper and pencil to make paper pattern, if you wish

Scissors

Large tray

Zipper-style plastic sandwich bag

1 POUR orange gelatin into bowl. Add 2½ cups boiling water to gelatin. Stir with rubber scraper until gelatin is completely dissolved, about 2 minutes. Pour into one of the 13 x 9-inch pans.

2 PREPARE lime gelatin in same way as orange gelatin. Put both pans into refrigerator to chill until firm, about 3 hours. After both pans of gelatin are firm, take them out of refrigerator. Put about 1 inch of warm water in sink. Dip **just bottom** of each pan into warm water for 15 seconds.

3 **LET** gelatin stand until thickened, 5 to 10 minutes. Gently stir in sliced bananas. Spray inside of mold with no-stick cooking spray. Pour gelatin mixture into mold. Put mold into refrigerator to chill until firm, about 2 hours. Take mold out of refrigerator.

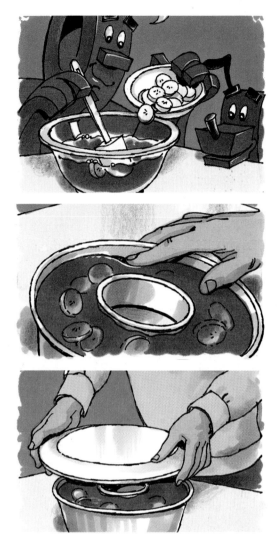

4 **PUT** about 4 inches of warm water in sink. Dip mold into warm water **just to top** of mold for 10 seconds. Dip your fingers in warm water. Gently pull gelatin from edge of mold with wet fingers.

5 **PUT** plate upside down on top of mold. Holding tightly, turn mold and plate over so mold is on top and plate is on bottom. (Have an adult help you.) Shake gently to loosen gelatin. Take mold off. Arrange fresh fruit inside or around mold, as you wish.

Makes 8 servings

TACO SALAD MOLD

INGREDIENTS

3 packages (4-serving size each) JELL-O Gelatin, Lemon Flavor
1 teaspoon salt
2½ cups boiling water
1 jar (16 ounces) taco sauce, medium flavor
3 tablespoons vinegar
1 teaspoon chili powder
1 package (10 ounces) frozen sweet corn, thawed, drained
No-stick cooking spray
Shredded lettuce, sour cream and tortilla chips, if you wish

EQUIPMENT

Medium mixing bowl
Measuring spoons
Measuring cup
Rubber scraper or large spoon
5-cup mold
Serving plate or tray

1 POUR gelatin into bowl. Add salt. Add 2½ cups boiling water to gelatin and salt. Stir with rubber scraper until gelatin is completely dissolved, about 2 minutes.

2 ADD taco sauce, vinegar and chili powder to gelatin mixture. Stir. Put bowl into refrigerator to chill until slightly thickened, about 1 hour. Take bowl out of refrigerator. Stir in corn.

If you do not have a mold, you can make the salad in a bowl.

3 SPRAY inside of mold with no-stick cooking spray. Pour gelatin mixture into mold. Put mold into refrigerator to chill until firm, about 4 hours.

4 TAKE mold out of refrigerator. Put about 4 inches of warm water into sink. Dip mold in warm water **just to top** of mold for 10 seconds. Dip your fingers in warm water. Gently pull gelatin from edge of mold with wet fingers.

5 PUT plate upside down on top of mold. Holding tightly, turn mold and plate over so mold is on top and plate is on bottom. (Have an adult help you.) Shake gently to loosen gelatin. Take mold off. Serve with shredded lettuce, sour cream and tortilla chips, if you wish.

Makes 10 to 12 servings

PUDDING POKE CAKE

<table>
<tr><td>

INGREDIENTS

1 pound cake loaf (about
   12 ounces)

1½ cups cold milk

1 package (4-serving size)
   JELL-O Instant Pudding,
   Chocolate Flavor

   Candy decorations, if you
   wish

</td><td>

EQUIPMENT

Serving plate

Wooden spoon

Measuring cups

1-quart shaker with a tight lid

Table knife

</td></tr>
</table>

1 REMOVE cake from wrapper and place it on plate. Poke 25 to 30 holes into top of cake with handle of wooden spoon.

2 POUR 1½ cups of cold milk into shaker. Add pudding mix. Put lid on shaker very tightly. Shake very hard for at least 45 seconds. (Be sure to hold top and bottom of shaker tightly.)

3 POUR about ¼ of the pudding mixture quickly over holes in cake. Tap cake lightly on counter so pudding will go down holes. Pour about ⅓ of the rest of the pudding over holes. Tap cake again.

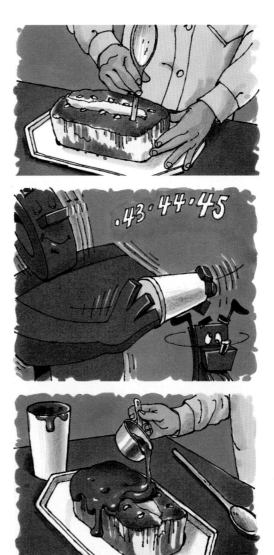

4 LET rest of pudding stand 2 minutes to thicken. Frost sides and top of cake with remaining pudding using table knife. Put cake into refrigerator to chill until serving time. Sprinkle with candy decorations, if you wish.

Makes 8 to 10 servings

COOKIES & CREAM PUDDING PIE

INGREDIENTS	**EQUIPMENT**
26 chocolate sandwich cookies 1½ cups cold milk 1 cup (½ pint) vanilla ice cream, softened 1 package (4-serving size) JELL-O Instant Pudding, Chocolate Flavor COOL WHIP Whipped Topping, thawed, for decoration, if you wish	9-inch pie plate Measuring cup Medium mixing bowl Wire whisk Zipper-style plastic sandwich bag Scissors

1 **PLACE** cookies on bottom and sides of pie plate. Cookies should cover plate evenly.

2 **POUR** 1½ cups of cold milk into bowl. Add ice cream. Beat with wire whisk until well blended. Add pudding mix. Beat with wire whisk until well blended, about 2 minutes. Let pudding stand for 3 minutes.

3 **POUR** pudding into cookie-lined pie plate. Put pie into refrigerator to chill until set, about 3 hours. To decorate, spoon whipped topping into zipper-style plastic sandwich bag. Squeeze extra air out of bag; close top tightly. Snip a small corner off bottom of bag with scissors. Squeeze bag gently to make design. Chill until serving time.

Makes 8 servings

crochet ripple

easy stripes

intermediate

finished measurements

60" x 76"/152.5 x 193cm

gauge

22 sts between points to 4"/10 and 8 rows to 6"/15cm over pat st using size J/10 (6mm) crochet hook.
TAKE TIME TO CHECK YOUR GAUGE.

afghan

With A, ch 319 for base chain.

Row 1 Dc in 5th ch from hook, 1 dc in next ch, *ch 2, sk 2 ch, 1 dc in each of next 2 ch, ch 2, sk 2 ch, 1 dc in next ch, work 1 dc, ch 2, 1 dc all in next ch for ascending point, 1 dc in next ch, [ch 2, sk 2 ch, 1 dc in each of next 2 ch] twice, sk next 2 ch for descending point, 1 dc in each of next 2 ch; rep from * across, ending last rep with sk 1 ch, 1 dc in last ch—there are 14 full descending points with ½ point at each end. Ch 3, turn.

Row 2 (RS) Drawing up lp of each dc to ¾"/2cm, sk first 3 dc, *[working over ch on previous row, work 1 dc in each of 2 sk ch of base-ch, ch 2, sk 2 dc] twice, work 2 dc, ch 2, 2 dc all in ch-2 sp of ascending point, [ch 2, sk 2 dc, working over ch, work 1 dc in each of 2 sk ch of base-ch] twice, sk next 4 dc of descending point (do not ch 2 between dc's over point); rep from * across, ending last rep with sk last 2 dc, 1 dc in top of beg-ch. Mark this row as RS. Ch 3, turn.

Row 3 Drawing up lp of each dc to ¾"/2cm, sk first 3 dc, *[working over ch, work 1 dc in each

of 2 sk dc on previous row, ch 2, sk 2 dc] twice, work 2 dc, ch 2, 2 dc all in ch-2 sp of ascending point, [ch 2, sk 2 dc, working over ch, work 1 dc in each of 2 sk dc] twice, sk 4 dc of descending point; rep from * across, ending last rep with sk last 2 dc, 1 dc in 3rd ch of turning-ch. Ch 3, turn. Rep row 3 for pat st.

Rows 4-7 With A, work 4 rows more, working to within last dc of row 7; to change color, yo, sk last 2 dc, insert hook in 3rd ch of turning-ch, yo and draw up a lp, yo and draw through 2 lps only, draw a lp of B through last 2 A lps on hook. Cut A and with B, ch 3, turn. Beg first set of stripes.

Row 8 (RS) With B, work across, changing to A in last dc. Cut B and with A, ch 3, turn.

Row 9 With A, work across changing to B in last dc. Cut A and with B, ch 3, turn.

Rows 10-15 Rep rows 8 and 9, 3 times more, changing to B in last dc of row 15. There should be 4 B stripes and 4 A stripes. With B, ch 3, turn.

Rows 16-22 With B, work 7 rows, changing to A in last dc of row 22. With A, ch 3, turn. Beg second set of stripes.

Rows 23-30 Beg with A, work 8 rows alternating colors every row, changing to A in last dc of 4th B stripe. With A, ch 3, turn.

Rows 31-37 With A work 7 rows, changing to B in last dc of row 37. With B, ch 3, turn. Rep rows 8-37 twice more. Do not change colors at end of row 37 on second rep. With A, ch 1, turn.

Finishing row (RS) Working dc's in usual manner, with A, draw up a lp in each of first 2 dc, yo and draw through all 3 lps on hook for dec, *1 sc in next dc, [working over ch, work 1 dc in each of 2 sk dc, 1 sc in each of next 2 dc] twice,

(continued on page 135)

materials

Perfect Match® by Caron®, 8oz/226g skeins, each approx 400yd/366m (acrylic)
5 skeins in #7747 powder blue (A)
4 skeins in #7707 soft peach (B)

Size J/10 (6mm) crochet hook
OR SIZE TO OBTAIN GAUGE

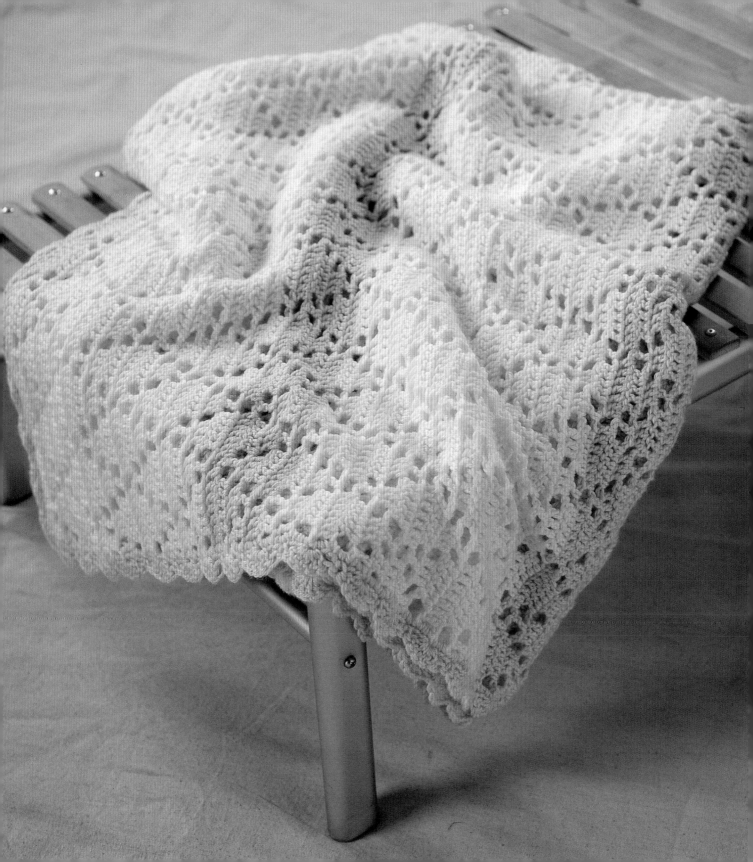

plaid tapestry

intermediate

finished measurements

50" x 64"/127 x 162.5cm

gauge

13 sts and 14 rows to 4"/10cm over sc using larger hook.
TAKE TIME TO CHECK YOUR GAUGE.

notes

1 Afghan is made of 6½"/16.5cm wide strips.
2 The strips are worked in sc using bobbins.
3 Wind colors A, B and C onto separate bobbins.

strip

(make 7)
With larger hook and A, ch 23.
Row 1 (RS) Sc in 2nd ch from hook and in next 5 ch, with B, sc in next 10 ch, with A, sc in last 6 ch—22 sts. Ch 1, turn.
Rows 2-4 Keeping to colors as established, sc across. Ch 1, turn.

Row 5 (RS) With D, sc across. Drop D. Go back to beg of row. Beg with A and rep rows 1 and 2. Drop Color A.
Row 8 Go back to beg of row (RS), pick up D and sc across. Drop D, pick up A.
Rows 9 and 10 Rep rows 1 and 2.
Rows 11-20 Work 6 sts using A, 10 sts using C and 6 sts using A. Work even for 10 rows. Rep rows 1-20 10 times, then rows 1-10 once. Fasten off.

finishing

Joining
From RS using smaller hook and D, work from bottom to top as foll: work a sl st ch between 2nd and 3rd st from each edge. Rep on all strips. Join strips from WS matching pat stripes

Edging
From RS with A and larger hook, join with 1 sl st at any point, ch 1, *sc in each sc and in each row; rep from * around, working 3 sc in each corner. Join rnd with sl st to beg ch. Ch 1, turn. Rep this rnd twice. **Last rnd** Working from left to right, sc in each st around. Join with a sl st in first sc. Fasten off.

materials

Wintuk® by Caron®, 3.5oz/6g skeins, each 150yd/137m (acrylic)
8 skeins in #3031 navy (A)
4 skeins each in #3032 rosewine (B), #3018 woodsy green (C) and #3021 oatmeal (D)

Size H/8 and J/10 (5 and 6mm) crochet hooks OR SIZE TO OBTAIN GAUGE

Bobbins

double diamond throw

finished measurements

48" x 63"/122 x 160cm

gauge

16 sts and 16 rows to 4"/10cm over sc using larger hook.
TAKE TIME TO CHECK YOUR GAUGE.

stitch glossary

FPtr (front post treble)
Yo twice, insert hook from front to back to front around post of stitch indicated, yo and pull up a lp even with last st worked and complete st.

Psc (picot sc)
Insert hook in next st, pull up a lp, [yo, draw through 1 lp on hook] 3 times, yo and draw through both lps on hook.

afghan

With larger hook, ch 166.

Row 1 (WS) Sc in 2nd ch from hook and in each ch across—165 sc. Ch 1, turn.

Row 2 Work 13 sc, mark last sc for center st, sc in next 48 sts, mark last st, sc in next 44, mark last st, sc in 48, mark last st, sc in last 12. Ch 1, turn.

Row 3 and all WS rows Sc in each st across. Ch 1, turn.

Row 4 Sc in first sc, (*FPtr around next st 3 rows below, sk 1, sc in next st, FPtr around next st 3 rows below, sk 1*, sc in next 7, **work dc around post of marked st in 2 rows below, sk 1, sc in next sc, work 1 dc around same marked st, sk 1, **sc

in next 7 sc*; rep between *'s) sc in 35; rep between **'s, sc in next 41; rep between **'s, sc in 35; rep between ( )'s, sc. Ch 1, turn.

Row 6 Sc in first st, (*FPtr around FPtr, sk 1, sc in next st, FPtr around FPtr, sk 1*, sc in next 6, **dc around post of dc, sk 1, sc in next 3, dc around dc, sk 1, **sc in next 6, rep between *'s), sc in next 34 sts, dc around dc, sk 1, sc in next 3, dc around dc, sk 1, sc in next 39; rep between **'s, sc in next 34; rep between ( )'s, sc. Ch 1, turn.

Row 8 Sc in first st, (*FPtr around FPtr, sk 1, sc, FPtr around FPtr, sk 1*, sc in next 5, **dc, sk 1, sc in next 5, dc, sk 1, **sc in next 5; rep between *'s) sc in next 33, dc, sk 1, sc in next 5, dc, sk 1, sc in next 37; rep between **'s, sc in next 33; rep between ( )'s. Ch 1, turn.

Row 10 Sc in first st, (*tr, sk 1, sc, tr, sk 1, *sc in next 4, **dc, sk 1, sc in next 7, dc, sk 1**, sc in next 4; rep between *'s), sc in next 14, Psc, [sc in next 17, rep between **'s, sc in next 17, Psc] twice, sc in next 14, rep between *'s, sc in next 4; rep between **'s, sc in next 4; rep between *'s, sc in last st, ch 1, turn.

Row 12 Sc in first st, *tr, sk 1, sc , tr, sk 1, *sc in next 3, **dc, sk 1, sc in next 9, dc, sk 1**, sc in next 3; rep between *'s, sc in next 13, Psc, sc, Psc, work [sc next 15, rep between **'s, sc in next 15, Psc, sc, Psc] twice, work 13 sc; rep between *'s, sc in next 3; rep between **'s, sc in next 3; rep between *'s, sc in last st. Ch 1, turn.

Row 14 Sc in first st, *tr, sk 1, sc, tr, sk 1, *sc in next 2, dc, sk 1, sc in next 6, mark last sc for center st, sc in next 5, dc, sk 1**, sc in next 2, rep between *'s, sc in next 12, Psc, [sc, Psc] twice, work [sc in 13, rep between **'s, sc in 13, (Psc,

(continued on page 135)

materials

Simply Soft® by Caron®, 3oz/85g skeins, each approx 163yd/150m (acrylic) 24 skeins in color of your choice

Size H/8 and I/9 (5 and 5.5mm) crochet hooks OR SIZE TO OBTAIN GAUGE

Open ended stitch markers

bouclé blue

intermediate

finished measurements

49" x 53"/124 x 134.5cm

gauge

16 sts and 20 rows to 4"/10cm over pat st using size 10 (6mm) needles.
TAKE TIME TO CHECK YOUR GAUGE.

stitch glossary

Tw2B
K into 2nd st on needle, then into 1st st on needle, slipping both sts off tog.

Tw2BP
P into 2nd st on needle, then into 1st st on needle, slipping both sts off tog.

pattern stitch

Row 1 (WS) Purl.
Row 2 P1, *Tw2B, p1; rep from * to end.
Row 3 K1, *Tw2BP, k1; rep from * to end.
Row 4 Knit.
Rep rows 1-4 for pat st.

afghan

Cast on 136 sts.
**Purl 3 rows (mark first row as WS).
Row 4 (RS) K1, *yo, SKP; rep from *, end k1.**
Rep last 4 rows 3 times more.
Next row Purl.
Next row P4, *M1, p3; rep from * to end—169 sts. Cont in pat st and work even until piece measures 49½"/125.5cm from beg, end with a RS row.
Next row (WS) K4, *k2tog, k3; rep from * to end—136 sts.
Next row K1, *yo, SKP; rep from *, end k1.
Rep from ** to ** same as above 4 times. Purl next 2 rows. Bind off all sts purlwise.
Side edging
From RS, pick up and knit 173 sts evenly spaced along side edge. Knit next row.
Next row K1, *yo, SKP; rep from *, end k1.
Rep from ** to ** same as above 4 times. Purl next 2 rows. Bind off all sts purlwise. Rep along opposite side edge.

materials

Softee Chunky by Bernat®, 3 ½oz/100g balls, each approx 164yd/150m (acrylic)
11 balls #40119 Denim

Size 10 (6mm) circular needle, 29"/73.5cm long OR SIZE TO OBTAIN GAUGE

alaskan nights

intermediate

finished measurements

42" x 66"/106.5 x 167.5cm

gauge

10 sts and 8 rows to 4"/10cm over sc using size N/15 (10mm) crochet hook and 2 strands of yarn held tog.
TAKE TIME TO CHECK YOUR GAUGE.

note

Use 2 strands of yarn held tog throughout.

afghan

With two strands yarn held tog, ch 152.

Row 1 Sc in 2nd ch from hook and in each ch across—151 sts. Turn.

Rows 2-5 Ch 1, sc in each sc across; turn. End of row 5, do not turn.

Row 6 Working from left to right, work reverse sc in front lp of each sc across, ch 1, do not turn.

Row 7 Working from right to left, sc in the back lp of each sc not worked in previous row, ch 1, turn.

Row 8 Sc in each sc across, ch 1, turn.

Row 9 (RS) Note Each cable is completed before the next cable is begun, you will reverse direction twice to complete each separate cable. Work as folls: *Sc in first st, make cable as follows: ch 3, sk 2 sts, sc in next st, turn, sc in each of the 3 chs, sl st in the sc before ch was begun, turn (cable made), holding the cable towards you, work 1 sc in each of the 2 sk sts below the cable, ch 3, sk the sc where the previous ch is

attached and the next 2 sts, sc in next st, turn, sc in each of the 3 chs, sl st in the sc before ch was begun, turn; holding the cable towards you, sc in 2 sk sts as before*; rep from * to * across, ending by working sc in last st (same sc used to attach last ch-3), ch 1 turn.

Row 10 Sc in first sc, sc in each of next 2 sc behind first cable, *work 2 sc in first sc behind next cable, sc in next sc behind same cable*; rep from * to * across, ending by working sc in first sc of prev row, ch 1, turn.

Row 11 Sc in each sc across, do not turn.

Row 12 Rep row 6.

Row 13 Rep row 7.

Rows 14-20 Sc in each sc across, ch 1, turn.

Row 21 (RS) Sl st in first sc, ch 3, in row 18, work a sl st around post of 4th sc as follows: insert hook at right of post from front to back and again to front at left of st, hook yarn and draw lp through and complete st as a sl st, ch 3, in row 20, sk 5 sc, sl st in next sc, *ch 3, in row 18, sk 5 sc, sl st around post of next sc, ch 3: in row 20, sk 5 sc, sl st in next sc*; rep from * to * across, (Do not turn, you will now be working from left to right across row just worked.) **ch 7, sk 5 sc as before, sl st in same sc where ch-3 was attached, working sl st over prev sl st**; rep from ** to ** across ending last rep by working a sl st in last sc of row 20 (same st where first sl st of row 21 was worked), ch 2, do not turn.

Row 22 (RS) *Sk st used to anchor ch-7, sc in each of next 5 sc sk in row 21, ch 1*; rep from * to * across keeping each ch-7 to RS of work, ending last rep by working sc in each of last 5 sc sk in row 21, sc in same sc used to attach last ch-3 in row 21, ch 1, turn.

(continued on page 136)

materials

Red Heart Super Saver by Coats & Clark™, 6oz/170g skeins, each approx 348yd/319m (acrylic)
14 skeins in #4313 aran fleck

Size N/15 (10mm) crochet hook
OR SIZE TO OBTAIN GAUGE

prairie star

experienced

finished measurements

54" x 77"/137 x 195.5cm

gauge

One motif to 4" x 6"/10 x 15cm using size I/9 (5.5mm) crochet hook.
TAKE TIME TO CHECK YOUR GAUGE.

notes

1 After the first motif is completed, all others are joined while working rnd 3.
2 Work and join center 6 A motifs first, then work outward foll diagram.

motif I

With A, ch 4. Join with a sl st to form a ring.
Rnd 1 Ch 1, [sc, hdc, dc, tr, ch 3, tr, dc, hdc] twice all in ring. Join with a sl st in first sc.
Rnd 2 Ch 5, dc in sc,*dc in next 3 sts, (3 dc, ch 4, 3 dc) all in ch-3 sp, dc in next 3 sts**, (dc, ch 2, dc) all in next sc; rep from * to **. Join with a sl st in 3rd ch of ch-5.
Rnd 3 See note. Ch 3, *work (dc, ch 3, dc) all in ch-2 sp, dc in next 2 dc, ch 1, sk next dc, dc in next 3 dc, ch 1, sk next dc, work (3dc, ch 5, 3 dc) all in ch-4 sp, ch 1, sk next dc, dc in next 3 dc, ch 1, sk next dc **, dc in next 2 dc; rep from * to **; dc in last dc. Join with a sl st in 3rd ch of ch-3. Fasten off.

motif II

With A, work rnds 1 and 2 same as for motif I.
Rnd 3 Ch 3, dc in ch-2 sp; ch 1, with WS together sc in ch-3 sp on motif I, ch 1, dc in same ch-2 sp on motif II, dc in next 2 dc; sc in next ch-1 sp, sk

next dc on motif in progress—join made; dc in next 3 dc, join, 3 dc in ch-4 sp, ch 2, sc in ch-5 sp on motif I, ch 2, 3 dc in same ch-4 sp on motif II; complete same as motif I—one side joined.
Note Check motif placement carefully. Some motifs will be joined beg at a ch-5 sp. Some motifs will join a ch-3 sp to a ch-5 sp. Foll diagram, join all motifs as foll: sc in a corresponding sp of a completed motif (the sc replaces one ch-st on the motif in progress). Where 3, 4, or 6 points come together, join at points by sc into the sc of a previous joining.

half motif

Ch 4. Join with a sl st to form a ring.
Row 1 (RS) Ch 1, (sc, hdc, dc, tr, ch 3, tr, dc, hdc, sc) all in ring; do not join; turn.
Row 2 Ch 3, dc in first 4 sts, (3 dc, ch 4, 3 dc) all in ch-3 sp, dc in next 3 sts, 2 dc in last sc; turn.
Row 3 (joining row) Ch 3, sc in ch-sp on completed motif, ch 1, dc in first 3 dc, join, dc in next 3 dc, join, 3 dc in ch-4 sp, ch 2 sc in sc of previous joining, ch 2, 3 dc in same ch-4 sp, join to next motif, dc in next 3 dc, join, dc in next 2 dc, dc in top of ch-3, ch 1, sc in ch-sp on completed motif, ch 3, sl st in top of ch-3 of row 2. Fasten off.

finishing

Edging
Rnd 1 With RS facing, join E in any st, ch 1, work 1 rnd sc evenly around, inc at outer points and dec at inner points to keep work flat. Join to first sc. **Rnd 2** Ch 3, work 1 rnd dc, inc and dec at points as before to keep work flat. Join rnd with a sl st in 3rd ch of ch-3. Fasten off.

(see chart on page 140)

materials

Red Heart Super Saver Solids by Coats & Clark™, 8oz/226g skeins, each approx 452yd/414m (acrylic)
2 skeins in #316 soft white (F)
1 skein each in #378 claret (A) and #633 dk sage (E)

Multicolor Red Heart Super Saver by Coats & Clark™, 6oz/170g skeins, each approx 348yd/319m (acrylic)
2 skeins in #303 painted desert print (B)

Red Heart Fiesta by Coats & Clark™, 6oz/170g skeins, each approx 330yd/302m (acrylic/nylon)
3 skeins in #6013 wheat (C)
2 skeins in #6631 lt sage (D)

Size I/9 (5.5mm) crochet hook
OR SIZE TO OBTAIN GAUGE

rainbow ripple

easy

finished measuremnts

56" x 66"/142 x 167.5cm

gauge

14 sts and 14 rows to 4"/10cm over pat st using size I/9 (5.5mm) crochet hook.
TAKE TIME TO CHECK YOUR GAUGE.

afghan

With F, ch 282.

Row 1 (RS) Sc in 2nd ch from hook, sc in next ch, [sk next ch, sc in next ch, working backwards, sc in sk ch] 7 times, 3 sc in next ch, [sk next ch, sc in next ch, working backwards, sc in sk ch] 7 times, *sk next 2 ch, [sk next ch, sc in next ch, working backwards, sc in sk ch] 7 times, 3 sc in next ch, [sk next ch, sc in next ch, working backwards, sc in sk ch] 7 times*; rep from * to * across to within last 2 ch across, sc in last 2 ch. Turn.

Row 2 Ch 1, sk first sc, sc in each of next 16 sts, 3 sc in next st, sc in each of next 14 sts, *sk next 2 sts, sc in each of next 14 sts, 3 sc in next st, sc in each of next 14 sts*; rep from * to * across to within last 3 sts, sc in next st, sk next st, sc in last st. Turn. Fasten off.

Row 3 Join D in first sc, ch 1, sk first sc, sc in next st, [sk next st, sc in next st, working backwards, sc in sk st] 7 times, sc in next st, *3 sc in next st, [sk next st, sc in next st, working backwards, sc in sk st] 7 times, sk next 2 sts, [sk next st, sc in next st, working backwards, sc in sk st] 7 times*; rep from * to * across to within last 18 sts, 3 sc in next st, sc in next st, [sk next st, sc in next st, working backwards, sc in sk st] 7 times, sk next st, sc in last st. Turn.

Rows 4-7 Rep rows 2 and 3 twice.
Row 8 Rep row 2. Fasten off. Turn.
Row 9 With F rep row 3.
Row 10 Rep row 2. Fasten off. Turn.
Row 11 With A rep row 3.
Rows 12-15 Rep rows 2 and 3 twice.
Row 16 Rep row 2. Fasten off. Turn.
Row 17 With F rep row 3.
Row 18 Rep row 2. Fasten off. Turn.
Row 19 With E rep row 3.
Rows 20-23 Rep rows 2 and 3 twice.
Row 24 Rep row 2. Fasten off. Turn.
Row 25 With F rep row 3.
Row 26 Rep row 2. Fasten off. Turn.
Row 27 With C rep row 3.
Rows 28-31 Rep rows 2 and 3 twice.
Row 32 Rep row 2. Fasten off. Turn.
Row 33 With F rep row 3.
Row 34 Rep row 2. Fasten off. Turn.
Row 35 With B rep row 3.
Rows 36-39 Rep rows 2 and 3 twice.
Row 40 Rep row 2. Fasten off. Turn.
Row 41 With F rep row 3.
Row 42 Rep row 2. Fasten off. Turn.
Row 43 With D rep row 3.
Rows 44-47 Rep rows 2 and 3 twice.
Row 48 Rep row 2. Fasten off. Turn.
Rows 49-168 Rep rows 9-48 3 times.
Row 169 With F rep row 3.
Row 170 Rep row 2. Fasten off.

finishing

Side edging

With RS of afghan facing, join F with a sl st in side edge of first row. **Row 1** Ch 1, making sure that work lies flat, sc in each row along side edge. Fasten off. Rep along opposite side edge.

materials

TLC Essentials by Coats & Clark™, 6oz/170g skeins, each approx 326yd/299m (acrylic)
3 skeins in #2316 winter white (F)
2 skeins each in #2220 butter (A), #2531 lt plum (B), #2672 lt thyme (C), #2772 lt country rose (D) and #2883 country blue (E)

Size I/9 (5.5mm) crochet hook
OR SIZE TO OBTAIN GAUGE

patchwork cross afghan

experienced

finished measurements

49" x 58"/124.5 x 147.5cm

gauges

16 sts and 16 rows to 4"/10cm over basic afghan st using size K/10 (6.5mm) afghan hook.
One block to 13" x 16"/33 x 40.5cm over basic afghan st using size K/10 (6.5mm) afghan hook.
TAKE TIME TO CHECK YOUR GAUGES.

block

(make 9)
With afghan hook and A, ch 45.
Row 1 (first half) Insert hook in 2nd ch from hook, yo, draw yarn through st, *insert hook in next ch, yo, draw yarn through st; rep from * to end—45 lps on hook.
Row 1 (second half) Yo, draw yarn through one lp on hook, *yo, draw yarn through 2 lps on hook; rep from * across (working backwards from left to right). **Note** One lp rem on hook and counts as first lp of next row. Rep row 1, first half and second half for basic afghan st.
Rows 2-45 Work in afghan st following chart, changing colors as indicated.
Row 46 Sl st in each vertical st across. Fasten off.
Edging
With RS facing and crochet hook, join B in upper RH corner st.
Rnd 1 Ch 1, **sc in each of first 5 sts, *sk next st, sc in each of next 5 sts*; rep from * to * across to within last 3 sc, sk next st, sc in next 2 sc, ch 1, sc in row-end st of each row down length, ch 1**; rep from ** to ** around. Join rnd with a sl st in beg sc.
Rnd 2 Ch 1, sc in beg sc, *ch 1, sk next sc, sc in next sc*; rep from * to* across to next corner ch-1 sp, work (sc, ch 2, sc) in corner ch-1 sp,**sc in next sc; rep from * to * across to next corner ch-1 sp, work (sc, ch 2, sc) in corner ch-1 sp**; rep from ** to ** twice more. Join rnd with a sl st in beg sc. Fasten off.
Rnd 3 With RS of block facing, join C in beg sc, ch 1,**sc in first 2 sc, dc in next corresponding sc 2 rnds below (rnd 1) pulling dc up to current level of work, sc in next sc, ch 1, sk next ch-1 sp, sc in next sc, dc in next corresponding sc 2 rnds below (rnd 1) pulling dc up to current level of work, sc in next sc*; rep from * to * across to within 3 sts from corner, ch 1, sk next ch-1 sp, sc in each of next 2 sc, work (sc, ch 2, sc) in corner ch-2 sp**; rep from ** to ** 3 times. Join rnd with a sl st in beg sc. Fasten off.
Rnd 4 With RS of block facing, join A in upper RH corner sc, ch 1, **sc in each of first 5 sts, *dc in next corresponding sc 3 rnds below (rnd 1) pulling dc up to current level of work, sc in each of next 3 sts*; rep from * to * across to next corner ch-2 sp, work (sc, ch 2, sc) in corner ch-2 sp**; rep from ** to ** 3 times. Join rnd with a sl st in beg sc.

finishing

Joining
With crochet hook and A, sl st blocks tog 3 wide by 3 long, using back lp of each corresponding st of rnd 4. When joining blocks tog, make sure that each junction of four blocks and all other corners are evenly spaced so design will not be distorted.

(continued on page 141)

materials

Red Heart Super Saver by Coats & Clark™, 8oz/226g skeins, each approx 452yd/414m (acrylic)
4 skeins in #313 aran (A)
2 skeins each in #633 dk sage (B) and #631 lt sage (C)

Size K/10 (6.5mm) afghan hook OR SIZE TO OBTAIN GAUGE

Size K/10 (6.5mm) crochet hook

retro chic

It is hip to be square—updating this classic
design is made easy with new yarns
in contemporary hues.

satin granny squares

easy

finished measurements
40" x 50"/101.5 x 127cm

gauge
One motif to 4½"/11.5cm using size I/9 (5.5mm) crochet hook.
TAKE TIME TO CHECK YOUR GAUGE.

motif
(make 99)
With MC, ch 4. Join with a sl st forming a ring.
Rnd 1 (RS) Ch 3 (counts as 1 dc), work [2 dc, (ch 2, 3 dc) 3 times] in ring, ch 2. Join with a sl st in 3rd ch of ch-3. Fasten off.
Rnd 2 Join A with a sl st in any ch-2 sp, ch 3 (counts as 1 dc), work (2 dc, ch 2, 3 dc) in same ch-2 sp, *1 dc in each of next 3 dc, work (3 dc, ch-2, 3 dc) in next ch-2 sp; rep from * twice more, end 1 dc in each of next 3 dc. Join with a sl st in 3rd ch of ch-3. Fasten off.
Rnd 3 Join MC with a sl st in any ch-2 sp, ch 3 (counts as 1 dc), work (2 dc, ch 2, 3 dc) in same ch-2 sp, *ch 1, sk next 3 dc, 1 dc in each of next 3 dc, ch 1, sk next 3 dc, work (3 dc, ch 2, 3 dc) in next ch-2 sp; rep from * twice more, end ch 1, sk next 3 dc, 1 dc in each of next 3 dc, ch 1, sk next 3 dc. Join with a sl st in 3rd ch of ch-3. Fasten off.
Rnd 4 Join B with a sl st in any ch-2 sp, ch 1, work 3 sc in same sp as last sl st, *[1 sc in each of next 3 dc, 1 sc in next ch-1 sp] twice, 1 sc in each of next 3 dc, 3 sc in next ch-2 sp; rep from * twice more, end [1 sc in each of next 3 dc, 1

sc in next ch-1 sp] twice, 1 sc in each of next 3 dc. Join with a sl st in first sc. Fasten off.

Joining 2 motifs
Work rnds 1-3 of motif.
Rnd 4 Join B with a sl st in any ch-2 sp, ch 1, work 3 sc in same sp as last sl st, *[1 sc in each of next 3 dc, 1 sc in next ch-1 sp] twice, 1 sc in each of next 3*, sc in next ch-2 sp; rep from * to * once more, work (2 sc, join with a sl st in 2nd sc in corner of adjoining motif, 1 sc) all in next ch-2 sp, [1 sc in each of next 3 dc, sk next 4 sc on adjoining motif, join with a sl st in next sc of adjoining motif, 1 sc in next ch-1 sp] twice, 1 sc in each of next 3 dc, work (1 sc, join with a sl st in 2nd sc in corner of adjoining motif, 2 sc) all in next ch-2 sp; rep from * to * once more. Join with a sl st in first sc. Fasten off.

Joining 3 motifs
Work rnds 1-3 of motif.
Rnd 4 Join B with a sl st in any corner, ch 1, work 3 sc in same sp as sl st, [1 sc in each of next 3 dc, 1 sc in next ch-1 sp] twice, 1 sc in each of next 3*, work (2 sc, join with a sl st in 2nd sc in corner of adjoining motif, 1 sc) all in next ch-2 sp, [1 sc in each of next 3 dc, sk next 4 sc of adjoining motif, join with a sl st in next sc of adjoining motif, 1 sc in next ch-1 sp] twice, 1 sc in each of next 3 dc*; rep from * to * once more, work (1 sc, join with a sl st in 2nd sc in corner of adjoining motif, 2 sc) all in next ch-2 sp, [1 sc in each of next 3 dc, 1 sc in next ch-1 sp] twice, 1 sc in each of next 3 dc. Join with a sl st in first sc. Fasten off.

materials
Satin by Bernat®, 3½oz/100g balls, each approx 163yd/149m (acrylic)
5 balls in #4143 lapis (MC)
4 balls in #4141 sapphire (A)
3 balls in #4110 admiral (B)

Size I/9 (5.5mm) crochet hook
OR SIZE TO OBTAIN GAUGE

4½"/11.5cm square of cardboard

Yarn needle

(continued on page 141)

wee granny squares

beginner

finished measurements

34" x 40"/76cm x 101.5cm

gauge

One basic granny square to 7½"/19cm using size G/6 (4mm) crochet hook.
TAKE TIME TO CHECK YOUR GAUGE.

basic granny squares

First color sequence

(make 10)

With A, ch 3. Join with sl st in first ch forming a ring.

Rnd 1 (RS) Ch 3 (always counts as 1 dc), work 2 dc in ring, [ch 3, 3 dc in ring] 3 times, ch 3. Join rnd with a sl st in top of beg ch-3.

Rnd 2 Sl st over to corner ch-3 sp, ch 3, work (2 dc, ch 3, 3 dc) in same sp, *ch 1, work (3 dc, ch 3, 3 dc) in next ch-3 sp; rep from * around, end ch 1. Join rnd with a sl st in top of beg ch-3. Fasten off.

Rnd 3 With the RS facing, join B with a sl st in any corner ch-3 sp. Ch 3, work (2 dc, ch 3, 3 dc) in same sp, *ch 1, work 3 dc in next ch-1 sp, ch 1, work (3 dc, ch 3, 3 dc) in next corner ch-3 sp; rep from * around, end ch 1, work 3 dc in next ch-1 sp, ch 1. Join rnd with a sl st in top of beg ch-3.

Rnd 4 Sl st to corner ch-3 sp, ch 3, work (2 dc, ch 3, 3 dc) in same sp, *[ch 1, 3 dc in next ch-1 sp] twice, ch 1**, work (3 dc, ch 3, 3 dc) in next corner ch-3 sp; rep from * around, end last rep at **. Join rnd with a sl st in top of beg ch-3. Fasten off.

Rnd 5 With the RS facing, join C with a sl st in any corner ch-3 sp. Ch 3, work (2 dc, ch 3, 3 dc) in same sp, *[ch 1, 3 dc in next ch-1 sp] 3 times, ch 1**, work (3 dc, ch 3, 3 dc) in next ch-3 sp; rep from * around, end last rep at **. Join rnd with a sl st in top of beg ch-3.

Rnd 6 Sl st to corner ch-3 sp, ch 3, work (2 dc, ch 3, 3 dc) in same sp, *[ch 1, 3 dc in next ch-1 sp] 4 times, ch 1**, work (3 dc, ch 3, 3 dc) in next ch-3 sp; rep from * around, end last rep at **. Join rnd with a sl st in top of beg ch-3. Fasten off.

Rnd 7 With the RS facing, join D with a sl st in any corner ch-3 sp. Ch 3, work (2 dc, ch 3, 3 dc) in same sp, *[ch 1, 3 dc in next ch-1 sp] 5 times, ch 1**, work (3 dc, ch 3, 3 dc) in next ch-3 sp; rep from * around, end last rep at **. Join rnd with a sl st in top of beg ch-3.

Rnd 8 Sl st to corner ch-3 sp, ch 3, work (2 dc, ch 3, 3 dc) in same sp, *[ch 1, 3 dc in next ch-1 sp] 6 times, ch 1**, work (3 dc, ch 3, 3 dc) in next ch-3 sp; rep from * around, end last rep at **. Join rnd with a sl st in top of beg ch-3. Fasten off.

Second color sequence

(make 5)

Work as for first color sequence using D for rnds 1-2, C for rnds 3-4, B for rnds 5-6 and A for rnds 7-8.

finishing

Joining

***Join tog 5 squares of first color sequence in one long strip. With RS facing, join E with a sl st in top right corner ch-3 sp. Ch 3 (counts as 1 dc), work 2 dc in same sp, *[ch 1, 3 dc in next

(continued on page 147)

materials

Babysoft by Lion Brand Yarn Co., 5oz/140g balls, each approx 459yd/420m (acrylic/nylon)
1 ball each in #157 Pastel Yellow (A), #106 Pastel Blue (B), #101 Pastel Pink (C), #156 Pastel Green (D), #100 White or colors of your choice (E)

Size G/6 (4mm) crochet hook
OR SIZE TO OBTAIN GAUGE

crochet ripple

(continued from page 12)

work 4 sc in ch-2 sp of ascending point, [1 sc in each of next 2 dc, working over ch, work 1 dc in each of 2 sk dc] twice, 1 sc in next dc, draw up a lp in each of next 2 dc over descending point, yo and draw through all 3 lps for dec; rep from * across, ending last rep by drawing up a lp in each of last dc and in 3rd ch of turning-ch, yo and draw through all 3 lps. Fasten off.

Finishing row on lower edge

From RS, join A with a sl st in 2nd ch of beg-ch in first point at right corner of lower edge, ch 1, work 1 sc in same ch as joining, 1 sc in next ch-1 sp; working along opposite side of base-ch, *work 1 sc in each of next 8 ch, draw up a lp in each of next 3 ch over descending point, yo and draw through all 4 lps on hook for dec, 1 sc in each of next 8 ch, work 4 sc in ch-2 sp of ascending point; rep from * across, ending last rep with 1 sc in ch-1 sp, 1 sc in first base-ch. Fasten off.

finishing

Steam lightly on WS.

prairie stripes

(continued from page 24)

side edge, work 3 sc in top right corner—482 sts. Join rnd with a sl st in first sc. Rnds 2 and 3 Ch 1, sc in each st around, working 3 sc in center st of each corner. Join rnd with a sl st in first sc. When rnd 3 is completed, join rnd with a sl st in first sc changing to B. Rnds 4-7 With B, rep rnd 2. When rnd 7 is completed, join rnd with a sl st in first sc changing to D. Rnds 8-11 With D, rep rnd 2. When rnd 11 is completed, fasten off.

double diamond throw

(continued from page 34)

sc) twice, Psc] twice, sc in next 12; rep between *'s, sc in 2; rep between **'s, sc in 2; rep between *'s, sc in last st. Ch 1, turn.

Row 16 Sc in first st, *tr, sk 1, sc, tr, sk 1*, sc, **dc, sk 1, work 5 sc, dc around marked st in 2nd row below, sk 1, sc, dc around same marked st, sk 1, work 5 sc, dc, sk 1**, sc; rep between *'s, sc in 11, Psc, [sc, Psc] 3 times, work [sc in 11; rep between **'s, sc in 11, (Psc, sc) 3 times, Psc] twice, sc in 11; rep between *'s, sc; rep between **'s, sc; rep between *'s, sc in last sc. Ch 1, turn.

Row 18 Sc in first st, *tr, sk 1, sc, tr, sk 1, *sc in next 2, **dc, sk 1, [work 3 sc, dc, sk 1] 3 times, **sc in next 2; rep between *'s, sc in 10, Psc, [sc, Psc] 4 times, work [sc in 11; rep between **'s, sc in 11, (Psc, sc) 4 times, Psc] twice, sc in 10; rep between *'s, sc in 2; rep between **'s, sc in 2, rep between *'s. Ch 1, turn.

Row 20 Sc in first st, *tr, sk 1, sc, tr, sk 1, *sc in next 3, **dc, sk 1, work 1 sc, dc, sk 1, 5 sc, dc, sk 1, 1 sc, dc, sk 1, **sc in next 3; rep between *'s, sc in 9, Psc, [sc, Psc] 5 times, [sc in 11, rep between **'s, sc in 11, (Psc, sc) 5 times, Psc] twice, sc in 9; rep between *'s, sc in next 3; rep between **'s, sc in 3; rep between *'s, sc. Ch 1, turn.

Row 22 Sc in first st, *tr, sk 1, sc, tr, sk 1, sc in next 4, **work dec dc as foll: yo, insert hook under next dc, yo, draw up lp, yo, draw through 2 lps, yo, insert hook under next dc, yo, draw up lp, yo, draw through 2 lps, yo, draw through 3 lps, sk 1, sc in 7, work dec dc**, sc in 4; rep between *'s, sc in 8, Psc, [sc, Psc] 6 times, [sc in 11; rep between **'s, sc in 11, (Psc, sc) 6 times, Psc] twice, sc in 8; rep between *'s, sc in 4; rep between **'s, sc in 4, rep between *'s, sc. Ch 1, turn.

Row 24 Sc in first st, *tr, sk 1, sc, tr, sk 1, *sc in 3, **dc around 2nd half of dec dc, sk next sc, sc, work dc around first half of dec dc, sk 1, work 5 sc, dc around 2nd half of dec dc, sk 1, sc, working under post, dc in dec dc in 2 rows below, sk 1, **sc in next 3 sc; rep between *'s, sc in 9, Psc, [sc, Psc] 5 times, [sc in 11, rep between **'s, sc in 11, (Psc, sc) 5 times, Psc] twice, sc in 9; rep between *'s, sc in 3; rep

between **'s, sc in 3; rep between *'s, sc. Ch 1, turn.

Row 26 Rep row 18.

Row 28 Sc in first st, *tr, sk 1, sc, tr, sk 1*, sc, **dc, sk 1, 5 sc, dc, sk 1, sc, dc, sk 1, 5 sc, dc, sk 1, **sc; rep between *'s, sc in 11, Psc, [sc, Psc] 3 times, [sc in 11, rep between **'s, sc in 11, (Psc, sc) 3 times, Psc] twice, sc in 11; rep between *'s, sc; rep between **'s, sc; rep between *'s, sc. Ch 1, turn.

Row 30 Sc in first st, *tr, sk 1, sc, tr, sk 1, *sc in 2, **dc, sk 1, 5 sc, work dec dc as in row 22, sk 1, sc in 5, dc, sk 1, **sc in 2; rep between *'s, sc in 12, Psc, [sc, Psc] twice, [sc in 13; rep between **'s, sc in 13, (Psc, sc) twice, Psc] twice, sc in 12; rep between *'s, sc in 2; rep between **'s, sc in 2; rep between *'s, sc. Ch 1, turn.

Row 32 Rep row 12.

Row 34 Rep row 10.

Row 36 Rep row 8.

Row 38 Rep row 6.

Row 40 Sc, *tr, sk 1, sc, tr, sk 1*, sc in 7, **dc, sk 1, sc, dc, sk 1**, sc in 7, rep between *'s, sc in 35; rep between **'s, sc in 41; rep between **'s, sc in 35; rep between *'s, sc in 7; rep between **'s, sc in 7; rep between *'s, sc. Ch 1, turn.

Row 42 Sc, *tr, sk 1, sc, tr, sk 1*, sc in 8, dec dc as on row 22, sc in 8; rep between *'s, sc in 36, dec dc, sc in 43, dec dc, sc in 36; rep between *'s, sc in 8, dec dc, sc in 8; rep between *'s, sc. Ch 1, turn.

Row 44 Sc, *tr, sk 1, sc, tr, sk 1*, sc in 9, mark last st, sc in 8, rep between *'s, sc in 37, mark last st, sc in 44, mark last st, sc in 36, rep between *'s, sc. Ch 1, turn. Rep rows 3-44 5 times, working tr on row 3 and end with row 3.

finishing

Left and right side edging

Work in ends of rows. From RS with smaller hook, sl st in first st, *Psc in next st, sl st, rep from * across.

Lattice Fringe

Row 1 From RS, join yarn in first sc, ch 1, insert hook in back of lp of ch just made, sc in ch (Double chain made—Dch); work 2 more Dch, *sk 3, sc in

double diamond throw

(continued from page 135)

next st, 3 Dch; rep from * across, end sc in last st. Turn. **Row 2** *Work 3 Dch, sc in ch sp; rep from * across. Turn. **Row 3** Rep row 2. Fasten off.

Fringe

Cut 5 16"/40.5cm long strands. Work on WS of afghan. Holding 5 strands tog, fold in half, pull lp through 3 Dch sp, pull ends up and tighten.

alaskan nights

(continued from page 38)

Row 23 Sc in each sc and in each ch-1 sp across, ending by working sc in turning ch sp, ch 1, turn.

Row 24 Sc in each sc across, ch 1, turn.

Row 25 (WS) Sc in each of first 3 sc, *attach ch-7 as foll: insert hook in next sc and then in back ridge of center of ch of ch-7; hook yarn, draw lp through and complete st as a sc, sc in each of next 5 sc*; rep from * to * across, ending last rep by working sc in each of last 3 sc, ch 1, turn.

Rows 26-30 Sc in each sc across, ch 1, turn, end of row 30, do not turn.

Rows 31-105 Rep rows 6-30 3 times.

Rows 106–117 Rep rows 6-17, end of row 117, do not turn, do not fasten off, work border.

Border

Rnd 1 With RS facing, working across width, ch 3 (first dc), *[dc in row-end st of next 15 rows, sk next row] 6 times, dc in each of last 6 dc across to corner, ch 2, working down length, dc in each sc across to next corner, ch 2*, dc in first row-end st of first row across width; rep from * to * around, join with sl st to top of beg ch 3. Fasten off.

floral water lily

(continued from page 40)

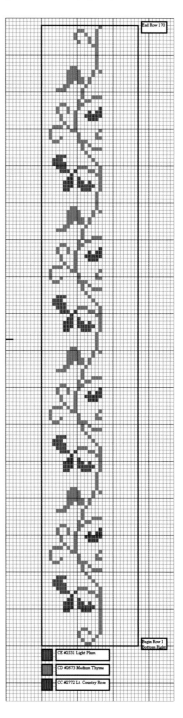

End Row 170

Begin Row 1
Bottom Eight

CE #2531 Light Plum
CD #2673 Medium Thyme
CC #2772 Lt. Country Rose

open windows set

(continued from page 44)

finishing

Referring to diagram, sew panels tog, alternating them as shown.

Edging

From RS with circular needle and MC, pick up and k 330 sts evenly along each side edge. Knit next 2 rows. Bind off.

Fringe

For each fringe, cut strands 10"/25.5cm long. Holding 3 strands tog and matching colors at end of each panel as shown, knot fringe evenly spaced across top and bottom edges.

pillow

(back and front make alike.)

With straight needles and MC, cast on 22 sts, with A, cast on 44 sts, with MC, cast on 22 sts—88 sts.
**Row 1 (RS) With MC, k22, with A, k44, with MC, k22.
Row 2 With MC, p22, with A, k44, with MC, p22.
Row 3 With MC, k22, with A, [k1, p1] 22 times, with MC, k22.
Rep rows 2 and 3 12 times more, then row 2 once.**
Row 4 With A, k22, with MC, k44, with A, k22.
Row 5 With A, k22, with MC, p44, with A, k22.
Row 6 With A, [k1, p1] 11 times, with MC, k44, with A, [k1, p1] 11 times.
Rep rows 5 and 6 5 times more, then row 5 once.
Row 7 With A, [k1, p1] 11 times, with MC, k12, with A, k20, with MC, k12, with A, [k1, p1] 11 times.
Row 8 With A, k22, with MC, p12, with A, [k2, p2] 5 times, with MC, p12, with A, k22.
Row 9 With A, [k1, p1] 11 times, with MC, k12, with A, [k2, p2] 5 times, with MC, k12, with A, [k1, p1] 11 times.

Row 10 With A, k22, with MC, p12, with A, [p2, k2] 5 times, with MC, p12, with A, k22.
Row 11 With A, [k1, p1] 11 times, with MC, k12, with A, [p2, k2] 5 times, with MC, k12, with A, [k1, p1] 11 times.
Rep rows 8-11 5 times more, then rows 8 and 9 once.
Row 12 With A, k22, with MC, p44, with A, k22.
Row 13 With A, [k1, p1] 11 times, with MC, k44, with A, [k1, p1] 11 times.
Rep rows 12 and 12 6 times more, then rows 12 once. Rep from ** to ** once more. Bind off in pat st.

finishing

Sew pieces tog along all but bottom edge. Insert pillow form; sew bottom edge closed.

Panel 1   Panel 2   Panel 1   Panel 2   Panel 1

lacy fern afghan

(continued from page 46)

finishing

Weave k1 edge of left panel to k1 edge of center panel. Rep for right panel.

Border

Row 1 With RS facing, sc evenly in each st across end to first point, ch 1, *sc in 15 sts, sc in center st of "V", sc in 15 sts to next point, ch 1; rep from * across to last point, sc evenly to edge. Turn. **Row 2** Ch 1 (for dc, ch 1), [sk 1 st, dc in next st] to 2 sts before first point, *sk 1 st, [dc, ch 1, dc] in next st, ch 1, dc in ch 1 sp; ch 1, [dc, ch 1, dc] in first of 15 sc, [sk 1 sc, dc in next sc] 6 times, sk 1 sc, center dec over next 3 sts, [sk 1 sc, dc in next sc] 6 times; rep from * across to last point, end [sk 1 st, dc in next st] across to last st. Fasten off.

handloomed homespun

(continued from page 48)

side edge of afghan, however, picking up 144 sts instead of 108 sts. Join border corners with flat seam. Weave in ends.

afghan panels

1	2	3	4	5	6
A	C	E	A	C	B
B	D	A	D	B	E
C	E	B	C	A	D
D	A	C	B	E	C
E	B	D	A	D	B
B	C	A	E	C	A

octagon afghan

(continued from page 56)

other octagons along side edges. Use one color marker for incs and another for decs.

Top and bottom edges

*With circular needle and CC, pick up and k16 sts across side of octagon on top edge, place inc marker, rep from * once, pick up and k16 sts across next side of octagon, place dec marker, rep placement of 2 inc markers, one dec marker 2 (5) more times across edge, end by placing 2 inc markers, pick up and k16 sts to end of row. **Next row (WS)** Knit. **Next row (RS)** Inc 1 st in first st of row, k to st before inc marker, inc 1 st in st before and inc 1 st in st after marker—2 sts made, cont across row, making incs before and after each inc marker and working to 2 sts before dec marker, k2tog before dec marker; k2tog after dec marker, cont across row working incs and decs where indicated, inc in last st of row. **Next row (WS)** Knit. Rep incs and decs on RS rows, k16 rows (8 ridges) of CC, 4 rows of MC, binding off across last WS row of MC. Rep for bottom edge.

Side edges

Pick up and k16 sts along one side of octagon, place inc marker, pick up and k16 sts along next side of octagon, place dec marker, [place 2 inc markers, 1 dec marker] 3 (5) times, ending placing 1 inc marker, work 16 sts to end of row. Work remainder of edging as for top edge. Rep for other side edge. Sew edging seams with flat seam. Weave in ends.

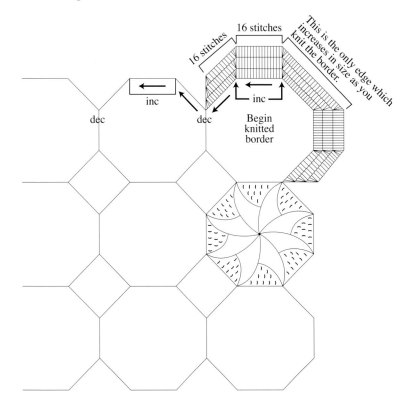

garden sprinkling can

(continued from page 60)

Edging

Rnd 1 From RS with crochet hook, join MC in upper right corner; ch 1, sc evenly spaced around, working 3 sc in each corner. Join with a sl st in first sc. Turn. **Rnd 2** Ch 1, *sc in next sc, bead st in next sc; rep from * around. Join with a sl st in first sc. Fasten off.

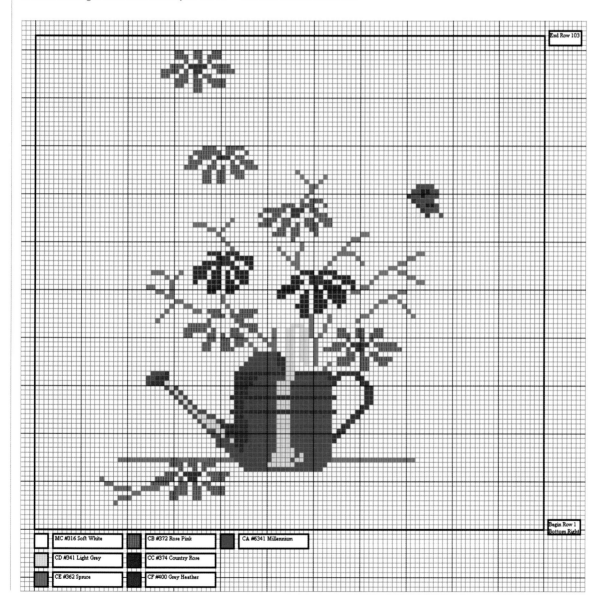

MC #316 Soft White	CB #372 Rose Pink	CA #6341 Millennium
CD #341 Light Grey	CC #374 Country Rose	
CE #362 Spruce	CF #400 Grey Heather	

End Row 103

Begin Row 1 Bottom Right

country blue

(continued from page 64)

Rnd 2 Join A in 2nd sc of any corner, ch 3 (count as 1 dc), work (1 dc, ch 2, 2 dc) in same joining st, *[sk 1 st, 2 dc in next st] rep between []'s up to next corner sc, work (2 dc, ch 2, 2 dc) in corner st; rep from * twice, rep between []'s to next corner. Join with a sl st to beg ch. Do not turn.

Rnds 3 and 4 Sl st up to ch-2 sp, ch 3, (count as 1 dc), work (1 dc, ch 2, 2 dc) in same ch-sp, *[sk next dc, 2 dc in sp between next 2 dc], rep between []'s to next corner, work (2 dc, ch 2, 2 dc) in corner ch-2 sp; rep from * twice, rep between []'s to next corner. Join with sl st to beg ch. Do not turn. At the end of rnd 4 join C. Do not turn.

Rnd 5 Ch 2, hdc in each dc, 4 hdc in each ch-2 sps. Join with a sl st to beg ch. Turn.

Rnd 6 Join A, ch 2, hdc around post of each hdc with no incs all around. Join with a sl st to beg ch. Turn.

Rnd 7 Join C, rep rnd 5.

Rnd 8 Rep rnd 6. At the end of rnd 8, fasten off A. Turn.

Rnd 9 Join B, 1 sc in each hdc, 3 sc in each corner. Fasten off.

finishing

Join in rows of 3 squares by 4.

Edging

From RS, join B in any corner. **Rnd 1** Ch 1, 1 sc in each sc all around, working 3 sc in each corner sc, end 2 sc in joining st, sl st in beg ch. Do not turn. **Rnd 2** Working from left to right, sc in each st around. Fasten off.

pillow

Work 1 square motif. Attach square to a 16"/40.5cm blue pillow.

prairie star

(continued from page 68)

assembly chart

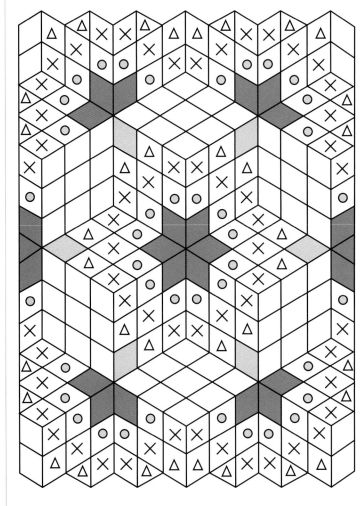

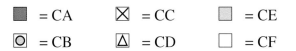

☐ = CA   ☒ = CC   ☐ = CE

◉ = CB   △ = CD   ☐ = CF

patchwork cross afghan

(continued from page 72)

Border

With RS facing and crochet hook, join B in upper RH corner sc. **Rnd 1** Ch 1, hdc in each st around (count joining seam as 2 sts), work (hdc, ch 2 hdc) in each corner ch-2 sp. Join rnd with a sl st in beg hdc. **Rnd 2** Ch 1, hdc in each hdc around, work (hdc, ch 2, hdc) in each corner ch-2 sp. Join rnd with a sl st in beg hdc. Fasten off. **Rnd 3** With RS, join C in upper RH corner hdc, ch 1, hdc in corner hdc, hdc in each of next 2 hdc, *ch 1, sk next hdc, **hdc in each of next 3 hdc*; rep from * across to within 2 hdc from corner, ch 1, sk next hdc, hdc in next hdc, work (hdc, ch 2, hdc) in corner ch-2 sp**; rep from ** to ** 3 times more. Join rnd with a sl st in beg hdc. Fasten off. **Rnd 4** With RS facing, join A in upper RH corner hdc, ch 1, hdc in corner hdc, hdc in each of next 3 hdc, dc in next corresponding hdc 2 rnds below (rnd 2) pulling dc up to current level of work, *hdc in each of next 3 hdc, dc in next corresponding hdc 2 rnds below (rnd 2), pulling dc up to current level of work*; rep from * to * across to within 2 hdc from corner ch-2 sp, hdc in each of next 2 hdc, work (hdc, ch 2, hdc) in corner ch-2 sp, **hdc in each of next 4 hdc, dc in next corresponding hdc 2 rnds below (rnd 2); rep from ** to ** twice more. Join rnd with a sl st in beg hdc. Fasten off. **Rnd 5** With RS facing, join B in upper RH corner hdc, ch 1, hdc in each of first 5 hdc, *ch 1, sk next dc, hdc in each of next 3 hdc*; rep from * to * across to next corner ch-2 sp, work (hdc, ch 2, hdc) in corner ch-2 sp, **hdc in each of next 5 hdc; rep from * to * across to next corner ch-2 sp, work (hdc, ch 2, hdc) in corner ch-2 sp**; rep from ** to ** twice more. Join rnd with a sl st in beg hdc. Fasten off. **Rnd 6** With RS facing, join A in upper RH corner ch-2 sp, **8 dc in corner ch-2 sp, sk next 3 hdc, sc in next hdc, sk next 2 hdc, 8 dc in next ch-1 sp, sk next 3 hdc, sc in next ch-1 sp*; rep from * to * across to within 4 hdc from corner ch-2 sp, sk next 4 hdc**; rep from ** to ** 3 times more. Join rnd with a sl st in beg sc. Fasten off. **Rnd 7** Ch 1, sc in each st around. Join rnd with a sl st in beg sc. Fasten off.

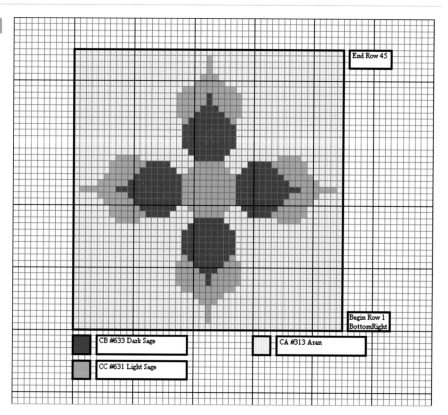

End Row 45

Begin Row 1 BottomRight

▩	CB #633 Dark Sage
▨	CC #631 Light Sage

▢	CA #313 Aran

retro chic

satin granny squares

(continued from page 76)

finishing

Join 9 motifs wide by 11 motifs long.

Tassel
(make 4)
Wind A around cardboard 30 times. Cut yarn leaving a long end and thread end through yarn needle. Sl needle through all lps and tie tightly. Remove cardboard and wind yarn tightly around loops 1"/2.5cm below fold. Fasten securely. Cut through rem lps and trim ends evenly. Sew a tassel to each corner.

amish blocks

(continued from page 78)

afghan

Foll diagram as indicated, matching all sides and corners, and inserting half-motifs where appropriate.

finishing

Border

Row 1 (RS) Join MC in any corner, ch 1, *work (sc, ch 3, sc) in corner, [ch 1, sk 1 st, sl st in next st] to next corner, (**Note** It may be necessary to sk more than 1 st on occasion to make sure work lays flat); rep from * 3 times; end sl st to first sc, sl st in ch-3 sp, ch 2. Turn. **Row 2** *Work 3 hdc in ch-3 sp, [2 hdc in ch-1 sp] to next corner, 3 hdc in ch-3 sp, ch 3; rep from * 3 times. Join with a sl st in 2nd ch of ch-2. Fasten off. Turn. **Row 3** Join A in any corner, working in back lps only, ch 3 , 2 dc in same sp, *ch 3, work 3 dc in same corner, dc in each hdc to corner, work 3 dc in corner; rep from * 3 times, ending last rep with ch 1, hdc in 3rd ch of first ch-3, ch 1. Turn. **Row 4** Sl st in corner sp, ch 2, hdc in corner sp, *hdc in front lp of each dc to corner**, work (2 hdc, ch 2, hdc) in corner sp; rep from * twice, then from * to ** once, in last corner, work 2 hdc, ch 2, sl st in 2nd ch of ch-2. Fasten off. Turn. **Row 5** Join B in any corner sp. Rep row 3. **Row 6** Rep row 4. Do not turn. **Row 7** Sc in front lp of each hdc around, (**Note** If work gets too bulky, change to a smaller hook). Fasten off.

christmas rose

(continued from page 86)

previous strip as before. Join second and subsequent motifs to side of previous motif and to side of motif of the previous strip; as motifs are joined on alternate sides, a square opening is formed; see diagram. Make 6 strips of 8 motifs.

square filler motif

(make 35)

With B, ch 4. Join with sl st to form a ring.

Rnd 1 Ch 1, work 8 sc in ring. Join with a sl st in first sc. Fasten off.

Rnd 2 Join D in any sc, work (beg cluster, ch 2, Cl) all in first sc, *ch 4**, sk 1 sc, work (sl, ch 2, Cl) all in next sc; rep from * around, end at **. Join with a sl st in top of beg Cl. Fasten off.

Rnd 3 Rep rnd 8 of flower motif.

Rnd 4 Ch 1, work (sc, ch 1, sc) all in first sc, *ch 1, sk next sc, [sc in next sc, ch 1, sk next sc] 4 times**, work (sc, ch 1, sc) all in next sc; rep from * around, end at **. Join. Fasten off.

Rnd 5 Rep rnd 10 of flower motif.

Rnd 6 Rep rnd 11 of second flower motif joining all 4 sides in square area between motifs.

finishing

Border

Rnd 1 With RS facing join C in any ch-3 corner sp, ch 1, *work (sc, ch 3, sc) in corner sp, ch 3, [sc in ch-3 sp, ch 3] 3 times; rep from * around working dec at joinings as foll: insert hook in joined ch-3 corner sp of first motif and pull lp through, insert hook in sl st of joining and pull lp through, insert hook in joined ch-3 corner sp of next motif and pull lp through; yo and draw through all 4 lps on hook. Join with a sl st in first sc.

Rnd 2 Sl st in ch-3 sp, ch 1, *(sc, ch 1, sc) in corner, ch 2, [sc in ch-3 sp, ch 2] 4 times; rep from * around except work ch 1 over dec instead of ch 2. Join. Fasten off.

Rnd 3 Join E in any corner ch-1 sp, ch 1, **work (sc, ch 1, sc) in corner sp, ch 2, *[sc in ch-2 sp, ch

2]; rep from * to corner; rep from ** around. Join.

Rnd 4 Sl st in ch-sp, *work (beg puff st, ch 1, ps) in corner ch-1 sp, ch 1, [ps in next ch-2 sp, ch 1] 6 times; rep from * around except work (ps, ch 1, ps) in each corner and work sts in brackets 4 times before and after each dec area sk ch-2 over dec. Join. Fasten off.

Rnd 5 Join C in any corner ch-1sp, ch 1, *(sc, 1, sc) in corner, ch 1, [sc in next ch-1 sp, ch 1] 7 times; rep from * around except sk ch-1 at dec

area and work sts in brackets 4 times before and after this area. Join.

Rnd 6 Sl st in ch-sp, ch 1, *(sc, ch 3, sc) in corner, ch 1, sc in next sc, ch 1, [(sc, ch 3, sc) all in next sc, ch 1, sc In next sc, ch 1] 3 times; rep from * around except work sts in brackets once to dec area, sk next (ch 1 and sc), work (sc, ch 3, sc) in ch-1 sp over dec area, sk next (sc and ch 1), sc in next sc, ch 1, work sts in brackets once to corner. Join. Fasten off.

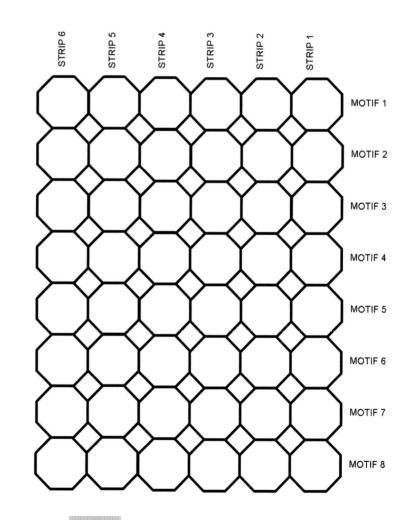

airplane blanket

(continued from page 94)

Top and bottom edging

From RS, with circular needle and E, pick up and k 175 sts evenly spaced along top edge. Knit next 2 rows. Bind off knitwise. Rep along bottom edge.

Side edging

From RS, with circular needle and C, pick up and k 213 sts evenly spaced along side edge. Knit next 2 rows. Bind off knitwise. Rep along opposite edge.

Chart I

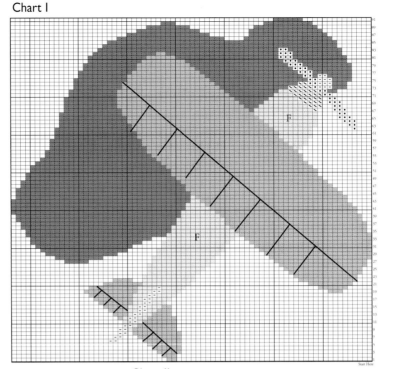

Key for Chart I

☐ = MC (Lt. Blue)

■ = Contrast A (Winter White)

▨ = Contrast B (Cardinal)

◿ = Contrast D (Gold)

▢ = Contrast F (Copen Blue)

⊡ = Contrast G (Aqua Sea)

⊟ = Contrast H (Navy)

╱ = straight st with H (Navy)

Chart II

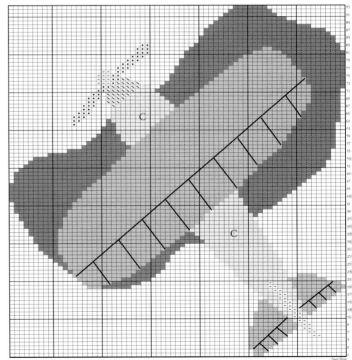

Key for Chart II

☐ = MC (Lt. Blue)

▨ = Contrast A (Winter White)

◪ = Contrast B (Cardinal)

▢ = Contrast C (Mauve)

▩ = Contrast E (Bright Royal)

⊡ = Contrast G (Aqua Sea)

⊟ = Contrast H (Navy)

╱ = straight st with G (Aqua Sea)

Chart III

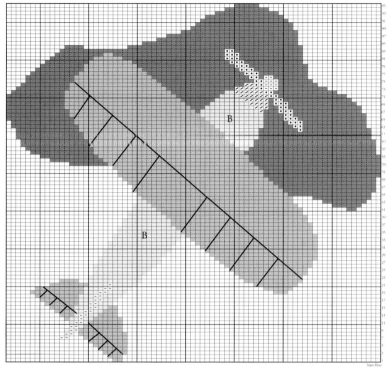

Start Here

Key for Chart III

□ = MC (Lt. Blue)

■ = Contrast A (Winter White)

▨ = Contrast B (Cardinal)

◪ = Contrast C (Mauve)

▦ = Contrast D (Gold)

⊡ = Contrast G (Aqua Sea)

⊟ = Contrast H (Navy)

╱ = straight st with H (Navy)

airplane toy

(continued from page 144)

materials

*Canadiana by Patons®, 3½ oz/100g balls,
each approx 201yd/184m (acrylic)
1 ball each in #30 med blue (MC),
#32 bright royal (B)
Small amounts of #26 mauve (A),
#34 navy (C), #5 cardinal (D)
and #81 gold (E)*

*One pair size 6 (4mm) needles
OR SIZE TO OBTAIN GAUGE*

Yarn needle

Polyester fiberfill

intermediate

finished measurements
13" x 13"/33 x 33 cm

gauge
21 sts and 27 rows to 4"/10cm over St st using
size 6 (4mm) needles.
TAKE TIME TO CHECK YOUR GAUGE

body
With MC, cast on 10 sts.
Row 1 (RS) *Inc 1 st in next st; rep from * to
end—20 sts.
Row 2 and all WS rows Purl.
Row 3 *K1, inc 1 st in next st; rep from * to
end—30 sts.
Next 3 rows Work in St st.
Row 7 *K2, inc 1 st in next st; rep from * to
end—40 sts. Beg with a p row, work even in St
st for 15 rows. With B, work even in St st for 30
rows. With MC, work even in St st for 8 rows.
Front shaping
Row 1 (RS) With E, *k2, k2tog; rep from * to
end—30 sts.
Row 2 and all WS rows Purl.
Row 3 With A, *k1, k2tog; rep from * to end—
20 sts.
Row 5 *K2tog; rep from * to end—10 sts.
Row 6 Purl. Cut yarn leaving a 12"/30.5cm long tail.
Thread tail in yarn needle and weave through rem
sts. Pull tight to gather, then fasten off securely.
Sew bottom seam leaving an opening for stuffing.
Stuff body; sew opening closed.

wing
(make 2)
With B, cast on 40 sts. Work even in St st for 4 rows.
Dec 1 st each side on next row, then every other
row 12 times more—14 sts. Bind off. Fold wing along
center of work and sew to cast-on edge. Sew side
edges tog. Stuff wings and sew cast-on edge to sides
of body, as shown.

airplane toy

(continued from page 145)

tail

With B, cast on 30 sts. Work even in St st for 4 rows. Dec 1 st each side on next row, then every 4th row 7 times more—14 sts. Bind off. Fold tail along center of work and sew to bound-off edge. Sew side edges tog. Stuff tail and sew cast-on edge to top back of body; as shown.

tail detail

(make 2)
With D, cast on 12 sts.
Row 1 (WS) Knit.
Row 2 [P2tog] 6 times—6 sts. Cut yarn leaving a long tail. Thread tail in yarn needle, then weave through rem sts. Pull tight to gather, then fasten off securely. Sew seam. Sew to sides of tail; as shown.

nose

With C, cast on 20 sts loosely.
Row 1 (WS) Knit.
Row 2 [P2tog] 10 times—10 sts. Cut yarn leaving a long tail. Thread tail in yarn needle, then weave through rem sts. Pull tight to gather, then fasten off securely. Sew seam. Sew to front of body leaving an opening for stuffing. Stuff nose lightly, then sew opening closed.

propeller

(make 2)
With C, cast on 20 sts loosely.
Row 1 (WS) K14, turn (leave rem sts unworked).
Row 2 Knit. Bind off all sts. Sew pieces to nose; as shown.

STRAIGHT STITCH

quilted squares

(continued from page 100)

motif III

(make 7)
Work as given for motif I, using C instead of A.

finishing

Referring to diagram, sew motifs into strips, then sew strips into blanket.

Edging

Rnd 1 Join MC with a sl st in top right corner, ch 3, work 4 dc in same sp, working in back lp only of each st to end of rnd, *1 dc in each st across to next corner; work 5 dc in next corner; rep from * twice more, end 1 dc in each st across to first corner. Join with a sl st in 3rd ch of ch-3. **Rnds 2 and 3** Ch 3, 1 dc in each dc across to next corner dc, *5 dc in next corner dc, 1 dc in each dc across to next corner dc; rep from * 3 times more. Join with a sl st in 3rd ch of ch-3. After rnd 3 is completed, fasten off. **Rnd 4** Join A with sl st in first corner dc, ch 3, work 4 dc in same sp, *1 dc in each dc across to next corner dc, 5 dc in next corner dc; rep from * twice more, end 1 dc in each dc across to first corner. Join with a sl st in 3rd ch of ch-3. **Rnd 5** Working from left to right, work 1 sc in each dc around (see illustrations). Join with a sl st in first sc. Fasten off.

easy as 1-2-3

(continued from page 104)

ing motif I and motif II. For side, sew 13 motifs tog, alternating motif II and motif I. Do not sew to blanket.

Inner edging

With hook, join MC with a sl st in first motif of bottom left corner of border granny square border, ch 1, *work 1 sc in each of next 9 dc across first motif, work 1 sc in joining sp between 2 motifs; rep from * to next corner. Dec in corner as foll: draw up a lp in corner 2 dc, yo and draw through all 3 lps on hook (sc 2tog made); ** rep from * to ** around, working sc 2tog across last and first sc. Join with a sl st in first sc.
Fasten off.

Outer edging

With hook, join MC with a sl st in any corner, ch 1, work 1 sc in each of next 9 dc across first motif, *work 1 sc in joining sp between 2 motifs, work 1 sc in each of next 9 dc across next motif; rep from * around, working 3 sc in each corner. Join with a sl st in first sc. Fasten off. Sew granny square border to center section.

wee granny squares

(continued from page 108)

ch-1 sp] to corner, in corner ch-3 sp work (ch 1, 3 dc, ch 3, 3 dc); rep from * around, end work (ch 1, 3 dc, ch 3) in first corner. Join rnd with a sl st in top of beg ch-3. Turn.

Row 1 (WS) Sl st in ch-3 sp, in first dc work sl st, ch 4 (counts as 1 dc and ch 1, [work 3 dc in next ch-1 sp, ch 1] across 44 times, sk 2 dc, dc in next dc until 2 lps rem on hook, with A yo and complete the dc (color change made). Turn. Fasten off E.

Row 2 With A, ch 3 (counts as 1 dc), 2 dc in first sp, (ch 1, sk 3 dc, 3 dc in next sp) 44 times; turn.

Row 3 With A, ch 4 (counts as 1 dc and ch 1), [work 3 dc in next ch-1 sp, ch 1] 44 times, sk 2 dc, dc in next dc changing to B. Turn. Fasten off A.

Rows 4-5 With B, rep rows 2-3 changing to C at the end of row 5. Fasten off B.

Rows 6-7 With C, rep rows 2-3 changing to D at the end of row 7. Fasten off C.

Rows 8-9 With D, rep rows 2-3 changing to E at the end of row 9. Fasten off D.

Rows 10-11 With E, rep rows 2-3. After row 11, fasten off E ***.

Rep from *** to *** for second set of 5 granny squares in first color sequence. Join tog 5 squares of second color sequence. Using second strip in the center, join one of the first strips to the side edge so that the colors from left to right on first are E, D, C, B, A and E. Join rem first strip to second so that the colors from right to left are E, D, C, B, A and E.

Edging

With RS facing, join E with a sl st in any corner.

Rnd 1 Ch 3 (counts as 1 dc), in same sp work (2 dc, ch 3, 3 dc), *ch 1, work 3 dc in next sp; rep from * around working (ch 1, 3 dc, ch 3, 3 dc) in each corner, end ch 1. Join rnd with a sl st in top of beg ch-3.

Rnd 2 Sl st to corner ch-3 sp, then rep rnd 1.

Rnd 3 Ch 1, sc in joining and in each of next 2 dc. Working 5 sc in each corner ch-3 sp, sc in each dc and ch-1 sp around. Join rnd with a sl st in first sc.

Rnd 4 Ch 3 (counts as 1 dc), dc in each sc around working 3 dc in 3rd sc of each corner. Join rnd with a sl st in top of beg ch-3. Turn.

Rnd 5 (WS) Ch 1, sc in each dc around working 3 sc in 2nd dc of each corner. Join rnd with a sl st in first sc. Fasten off.

clustered bobbles

(continued from page 110)

combination) to any ch-1 sp, ch 6 (counts as 1 dc and ch-3 base for cluster), work Cl st in 3rd ch from hook, ch 1, *sc in next ch-1 sp, ch 1, dc in next ch-1 sp, ch 3, work Cl st in 3rd ch from hook, ch 1 **; rep from * to ** around. Join with a sl st in 3rd ch of ch-6. Fasten off.

assembly chart

1	2	1	2	1	2	1	2	1	2	1	2
2	1	2	1	2	1	2	1	2	1	2	1
1	2	1	2	1	2	1	2	1	2	1	2
2	1	2	1	2	1	2	1	2	1	2	1
1	2	1	2	1	2	1	2	1	2	1	2
2	1	2	1	2	1	2	1	2	1	2	1
1	2	1	2	1	2	1	2	1	2	1	2
2	1	2	1	2	1	2	1	2	1	2	1
1	2	1	2	1	2	1	2	1	2	1	2
2	1	2	1	2	1	2	1	2	1	2	1
1	2	1	2	1	2	1	2	1	2	1	2
2	1	2	1	2	1	2	1	2	1	2	1

cradle comforts

(continued from page 114)

finishing

Sew strips tog, alternating strip A and B; as shown.

Top and bottom edging

With circular needle and MC, pick up and k 153 sts across top edge. **Row 1 (WS)** P1, *k1, p1; rep from * to end. **Row 2** K1, inc 1 st in next st purlwise, *k1, p1; rep from * to last 3 sts, end k1, inc 1 st in next st purlwise, k1. **Row 3** P1, k2, *p1, k1; rep from * to last 3 sts, end k2, p1. **Row 4** K1, inc 1 st in next st purlwise, *p1, k1; rep from * to last 3 sts, end p1, inc 1 st in next st purlwise, k1. Rep rows 1-4 until edging measures 2"/5cm from beg, end with a WS row. Bind off loosely in rib. Rep along bottom edge.

Side edging

With circular needle and MC, pick up and knit 185 sts along side edge. Work same as for top and bottom edging. Rep along opposite side edge. Sew edging tog at corners.

Chart II

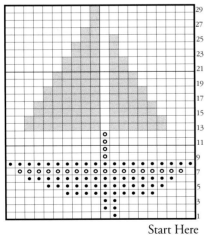

Start Here

Chart I

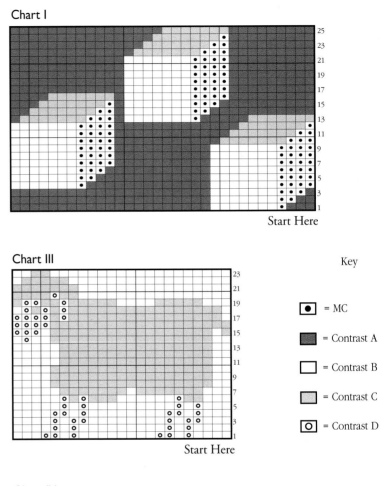

Start Here

Chart III

Key

● = MC

= Contrast A

= Contrast B

= Contrast C

○ = Contrast D

Start Here

Chart IV

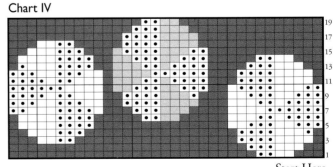

Start Here

counting sheep

(continued from page 116)

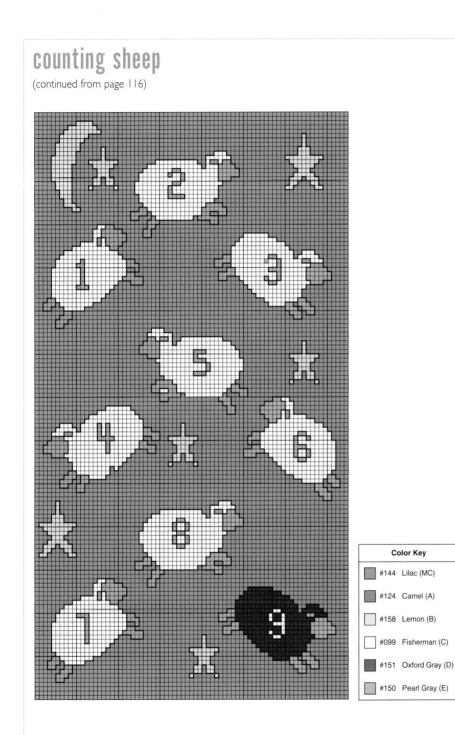

Color Key	
■	#144 Lilac (MC)
▨	#124 Camel (A)
▨	#158 Lemon (B)
□	#099 Fisherman (C)
■	#151 Oxford Gray (D)
▨	#150 Pearl Gray (E)

autumn treasure

(continued from page 120)

using D instead of MC.

Small square 4
(make 2 for each block A)
Work as for small square 1 until last rnd and using E instead of MC.

Assembling
Assemble squares as shown in diagram to form block A. From RS, join B in top right corner and work 1 rnd of sc around outer edge, working 3 sc in each corner. Join with sl st to first sc. Fasten off.

block B

(make 15)

Note To change color, work to last 2 lps on hook. Draw loop in next color through 2 lps on hook to complete st and proceed in next color. With E, ch 42 loosely.

Foundation row (RS) Dc in 4th ch from hook, 1 dc in each of next 2 ch, *with B, 1 dc in each of next 4 ch, with E, 1 dc in each of next 4 ch; rep from * twice more, with B, 1 dc in each of last 4 ch, 40 dc. Ch 3, turn.

Row 1 Sk first dc, 1 dc in each of next 3 dc, *with E, 1 dc in each of next 4 dc, with B, 1 dc in each of next 4 dc; rep from * twice more, with E, 1 dc in each of next 4 dc. With D, ch 3, turn.

Row 2 Sk first dc, 1 dc in each of next 3 dc, *with D, 1 dc in each of next 4 dc, with B, 1 dc in each of next 4 dc; rep from * twice more, with D, 1 dc in each of next 4 dc. Ch 3, turn.

Row 3 Sk first dc, 1 dc in each of next 3 dc, *with B, 1 dc in each of next 4 dc, with D, 1 dc in each of next 4 dc; rep from * twice more, with B, 1 dc in each of next 4 dc. With E, ch 3, turn.

Row 4 Sk first dc, 1 dc in each of next 3 dc, *with C, 1 dc in each of next 4 dc, with E, 1 dc in each of next 4 dc; rep from * twice more, with C, 1 dc in each of next 4 dc. Ch 3, turn.

Row 5 Sk first dc, 1 dc in each of next 3 dc, *with E, 1 dc in each of next 4 dc, with C, 1 dc in each of next 4 dc; rep from * twice more, with E, 1 dc in each of next 4 dc. With C, ch 3, turn.

autumn treasure

(continued from page 149)

Row 6 Sk first dc, I dc in each of next 3 dc, *with D, I dc in each of next 4 dc, with C, I dc in each of next 4 dc; rep from * twice more, with D, I dc in each of next 4 dc. Ch 3, turn.
Row 7 Sk first dc, I dc in each of next 3 dc, *with C, I dc in each of next 4 dc, with D, I dc in each of next 4 dc; rep from * twice more, with C, I dc in each of next 4 dc. With E, ch 3, turn.
Row 8 Sk first dc, I dc in each of next 3 dc, *with B, I dc in each of next 4 dc, with E, I dc in each of next 4 dc; rep from * twice more, with B, I dc in each of next 4 dc. Ch 3, turn. Rep rows 1-8 once more, then row I once omitting turning ch at end of last row. Fasten off.

finishing

Assemble blocks A and B as shown in diagram II.
Edging
Rnd I With RS facing, join B with a sl st in any corner; ch I, work 3 sc in same sp, cont to sc evenly around, working 3 sc in each corner. Join MC with sl st in first sc. Cut B. **Rnd 2** Ch I, sc in each sc around, working 3 sc in corner sc. Join with sl st in first sc. **Rnd 3** Ch I, working from left to right, work I sc in each sc around (see illustrations below). Join with sl st in first sc. Fasten off.

Block A

Large Square		Small Square 1	Small Square 2
		Small Square 3	Small Square 4
Small Square 1	Small Square 2	Large Square	
Small Square 3	Small Square 4		

A	B	A	B	A
B	A	B	A	B
A	B	A	B	A
B	A	B	A	B
A	B	A	B	A
B	A	B	A	B

commemorative police throw

(continued from page 124)

strips to motifs. Use long strips to connect three panels.

finishing
Top and bottom borders
From RS with circular needle and MC, pick up and k 188 sts along top of afghan. Work in rib pat for 6 rows, inc I st each side every other row 2 times—192 sts. Bind off in rib pat. Rep for bottom of afghan.
Side borders
From RS with circular needle and MC, pick up and k 276 sts along side of afghan. Work in rib pat same as top border—280 sts. Bind off in rib pat. Sew corner seams.
Whistle cord
With MC and crochet hook, make a chain st cord following photo for placement.

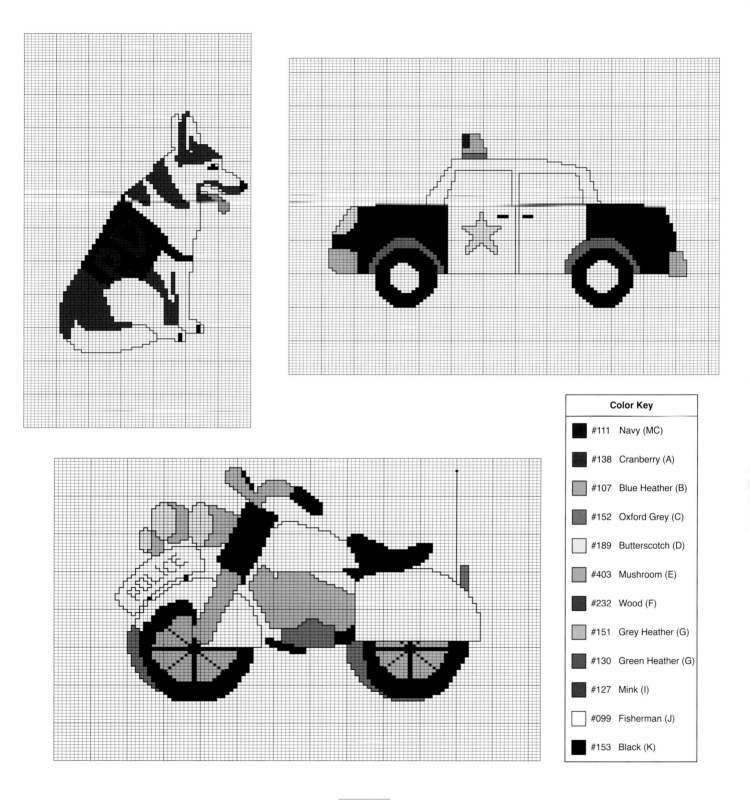

Color Key

■	#111	Navy (MC)
■	#138	Cranberry (A)
■	#107	Blue Heather (B)
■	#152	Oxford Grey (C)
□	#189	Butterscotch (D)
■	#403	Mushroom (E)
■	#232	Wood (F)
■	#151	Grey Heather (G)
■	#130	Green Heather (G)
■	#127	Mink (I)
□	#099	Fisherman (J)
■	#153	Black (K)

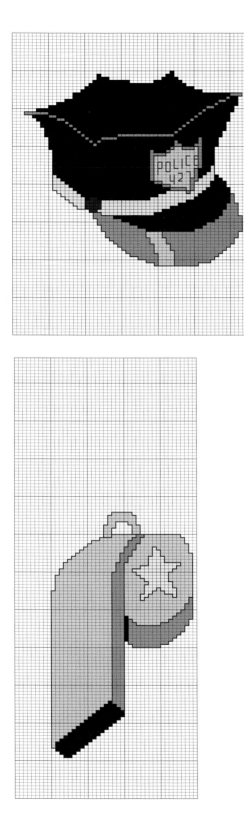

commemorative fireman throw

(continued from page 126)

embroidery

Working in cross stitch, embroider all panels by centering charts for motif and working in colors as indicated.

vertical panels

Work all panels with D.

Bottom

With afghan hook, ch 9 and work 52 rows BAS. Sew between Fireman's Hat and Fire Hose panels.

Middle

(make 2)

With afghan hook, ch 9 and work 104 rows BAS, sew one between Fire Hydrant and Firehouse, the other between Firehouse and Dalmation panels.

Top

With afghan hook, ch 9 and work 70 rows BAS. Sew between Firetruck and Fire Alarm panels.

horizontal panels

Work all panels with D.

Top

With afghan hook, pick up 194 sts and work 9 rows BAS.

Middle

With afghan hook, pick up 194 sts and work 9 rows BAS. Sew to top panel.

Bottom

With afghan hook, pick up 194 sts and work 9 rows BAS. Sew to middle panel. Rotate afghan and pick up 194 sts across bottom edge. Work 9 rows BAS.

finishing

Edging

With crochet hook, sc evenly around afghan, working 3 sc in each corner. **Picot Row** *Work 5 sc, ch 3, sl st into top of last sc; rep from *, working 3 sc in each corner.

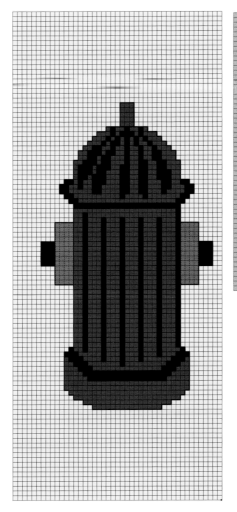

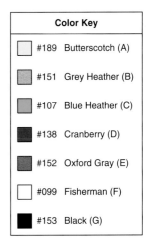

Color Key		
	#189	Butterscotch (A)
	#151	Grey Heather (B)
	#107	Blue Heather (C)
	#138	Cranberry (D)
	#152	Oxford Gray (E)
	#099	Fisherman (F)
	#153	Black (G)

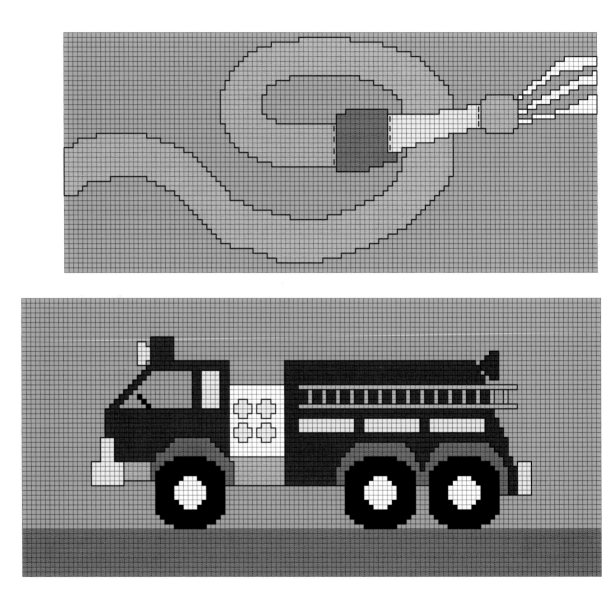

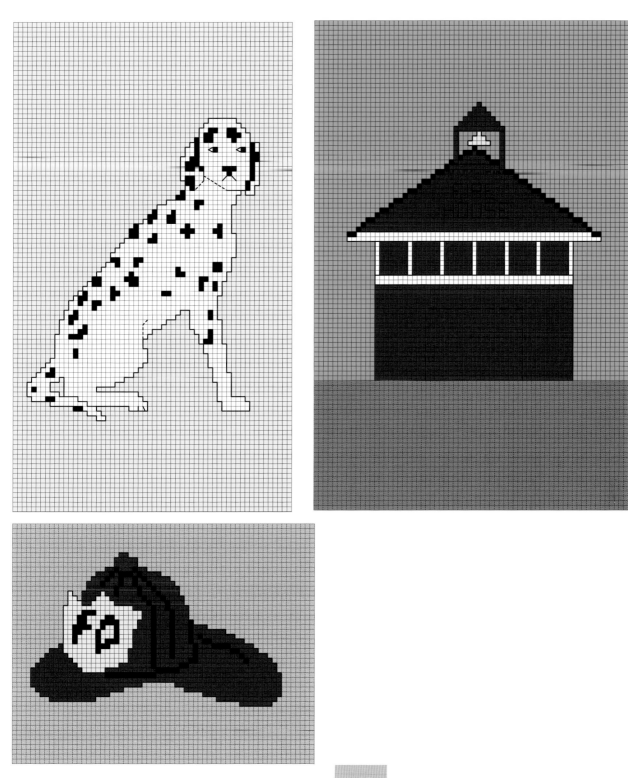

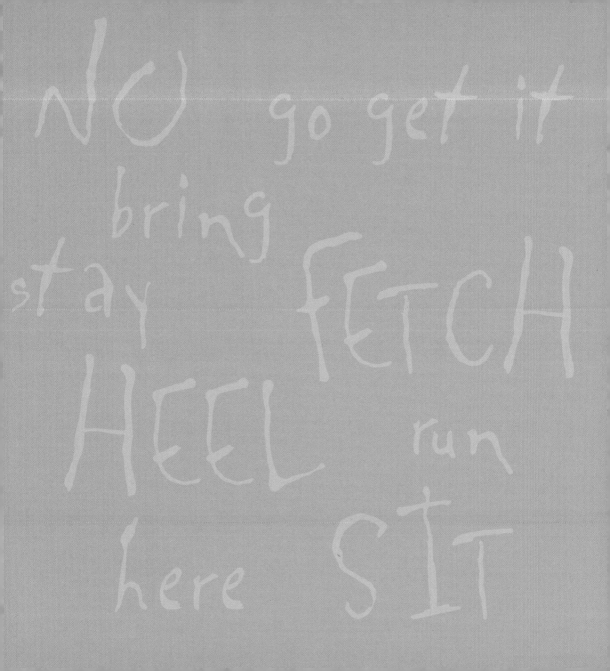

Growing Up

My Dog's First Birthday

A dog is like an eternal Peter Pan, a child who never grows old and who therefore is always available to be loved.   —Aaron Katcher

This Is No Ordinary Dog

Favorite Possessions

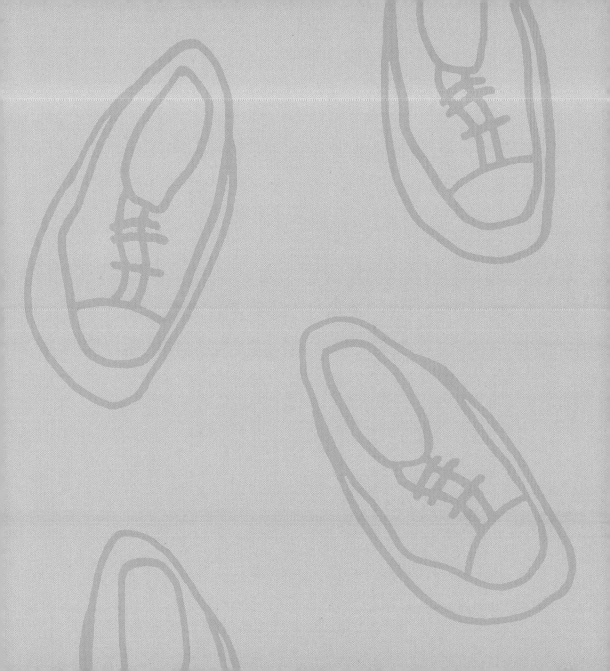